THE INVESTOR'S GUIDE TO U.S. SILVER STOCKS

By James E. Ryan

Sterling
Sunshine
American

Northwest Silver Press
Bellevue, Washington

This book is dedicated
to the serious investor
who wants to make money
in silver stocks.

Copyright ©1983 by James E. Ryan
All rights reserved
Manufactured in the U.S.A.
Published by Northwest Silver Press
   3 Lummi Key
   Bellevue, Washington 98006

ISBN 0-9610202-0-2

FOREWORD

Many books have been written about silver, but to my knowledge this book is the first good book with information about silver stocks that have an excellent chance for growth. You will find listed in this book companies that have a good chance for profit with limited risk. The underlying values of the companies reflected merit consideration.

I believe that Jim Ryan has done an important service in clearly developing information on silver mining companies often overlooked by the investment public.

PAUL SARNOFF
Vice President, Paine Webber, Jackson & Curtis
Director, Paine Webber Metals Unit

Mr. Sarnoff is an eminent authority on silver, the author of "The Silver Bulls" (see Appendix) and many other articles on the subject.

ACKNOWLEDGEMENTS

I wish to acknowledge and thank the many clients, friends, officers and directors of silver mining companies, brokers, analysts and financial writers who encouraged me to write this book.

In particular my appreciation and thanks go out to Ben Harrison, Elva Hallstein, Harry F. Magnuson, Wofford Conrad, Michael Boswell, Philip Lindstrom, Merle Dowd, Anne Dowd and Valerie Fitzsimonds for all their help and thoughtful and worthwhile suggestions without which this book could not have been written.

CONTENTS

PREFACE

Interest in the precious metals for investment and speculative purposes on the part of the general public throughout the world is exploding.

This is happening, of course, because of a growing distrust of all governments and the paper money they print.

Many investors, having invested in silver, gold and other hard assets, are also buying commodity futures and stocks related to the precious metals.

Those who have invested in stocks have probably found a total void when it came to getting information on this type of investment. Neither the New York Stock Exchange firms, *Standard & Poor's, Moody's* or any of the general statistical services follow gold or silver stocks to any degree.

So, if you have asked your broker recently for information or advice regarding this type of investment, undoubtedly you received a blank look or mumbled words to the effect, "We don't like silver stocks because they are too speculative."

Whatever the reasons your broker has given you, they are beside the point. If you are interested in buying silver stocks or in finding which ones to buy, you are entitled to be able to do just that. So that is the reason why this book was written.

I have attempted to provide a compendium covering a special category of stock—namely, the silver stocks, including all the "penny stocks." I hope this manual will help whether you are a broker, advisor and/or an investor to make more intelligent and profitable decisions than you could otherwise make.

JAMES E. RYAN

INTRODUCTION

At the writing of this book, the prices of precious metals and of silver in particular are advancing rapidly.

Most of the silver stocks covered in the text will be much higher by the time the reader has had a chance to check them out or even take a position in any of them. Some of the companies will probably even have been merged or bought out.

Life does go on, and obviously nothing is forever—so it will be academic whether you bought silver and/or the related stock when silver was $5 per ounce or $20 per ounce. Silver will in all probability go over its old high of $51, and the stocks will go with it.

As things change and as the need arises, this text will be updated—most likely each year.

I hope each reader finds this manual to be not only informative and profitable but also a useful aid in helping to navigate successfully the uncharted economic seas of the world today.

1

THE SILVER SITUATION TODAY

WHY SILVER STOCKS ARE ATTRACTING INVESTORS' ATTENTIONS

T HE roller coaster ride is continuing," as Paul Sarnoff has pointed out in his recent article on the silver situation today, "and it may be offering a fabulous buying opportunity in 1982–1983 for those willing to get in at the bottom of the curve."*

Everyone knows now that silver started from around $6, went over $50 and back down to $5 and, as of this writing, up to just under $10 per ounce. Now there are many prognostications of it's going over $100 per ounce. This is no enigma. The justification for these predictions is extensive.

At the recent bottom of the silver market, the U.S. government suspended any further sales from the strategic stockpile (136 million ounces remaining). Most of the silver mines in the U.S. shut down because the price of silver had fallen below the cost of bringing the metal to market at a profit.

Internationally, Peru, one of the major producers of silver in the western world, also placed a temporary moratorium on silver sales. Mexico, because of its financial problems plus serious and widespread social unrest, has seen its silver production decline. Canadian silver producers have also been on the sidelines for the same reasons.

Poland, the largest of Eastern block producers, has experienced loss of production because of deep seated resistance against the communist regime running the country. The USSR because of the above

*Moneymakers. "Hi Ho Silver Rides Again," Paul Sarnoff, Feb./Mar. 1982.

plus its expanded defense needs has now become a major importer of silver.

The often dredged up "old chestnut" that the Hunts' silver poses a threat to higher prices no longer exists because of their successful long-term refinancing of the 163 million ounces remaining.

Many experts today are also pointing to sharply increased consumption by the Peoples Republic of China resulting in a big jump in their importing of silver. Those same experts see a world shortfall of 400 million ounces of silver in the next three years when the one billion Chinese start to consume ½ ounce of silver per capita.

Along with all the aforementioned factors affecting the price of silver, we of course have investors and speculators alike again fleeing from paper money because of distrust of government.

Put this all together, and you have a rapidly expanding shortfall between consumption and production that will literally put the price of silver into orbit. By this I mean—*silver over $50 per ounce within one year!*

This brings us back to why silver stocks are attracting investors' attention.

Many people aware of what is happening to silver are buying bullion. Others are playing the commodity futures market, but the vast majority are starting to buy the silver stocks.

Those who choose this route are doing it because they are aware that stocks reflect first the profit possibilities within a particular industry—in this case, silver mining.

Stocks of the silver mining companies will tend to lead the market (*i.e.,* the price of silver), and investors also find it more convenient to buy and sell the shares rather than the bullion.

With silver having reached the bottom, it also was obvious that the stocks reflecting this situation must also be on the bargain counter. So, the move has started. It will develop into a stampede quickly, and it will be of long duration.

Those investors who share similar views would be wise in establishing positions in silver stock as expeditiously as possible.

2

THE SILVER STOCKS

As POINTED out by the title, the purpose of this book is principally to cover the silver stocks of the United States.

The need for such a manual has been obvious ever since interest has again come into silver and the other precious metals.

Even though there is information available on the larger silver mining companies such as Sunshine Mining Company and Hecla Mining Company, there has been very little available generally on the smaller ones.

Investors seeking information on any silver stock have discovered almost total ignorance on the part of stockbrokers on the subject.

This chapter will help to rectify this situation and give the interested reader a sound basis for reaching some sound conclusions regarding the silver mining stocks.

Silver stocks come in two sizes—big ones and little ones. The big ones such as Sunshine, Hecla, Callahan, and others, are not only high priced stocks, but also in general have larger capitalization (*i.e.,* the number of shares outstanding). Therefore, it is more difficult for their shares to move up as fast as their counterparts (*i.e.,* the little ones with fewer shares outstanding).

When an industry gets "hot" from an investment standpoint or for whatever reasons, the stocks representing it all go up more or less. Usually, however, the lower priced issues move up easier, faster and higher percentagewise than do the higher priced stocks. Physical laws of nature obviously apply to stock prices also.

Fortune Magazine in an article titled "Giant Payoffs From Midget Stocks" (February, 1981) arrived at the same conclusion and further pointed out that nondividend paying stocks also outperform dividend paying stocks for similar reasons. I mentioned this because one should not buy any silver stocks on the basis of a dividend return.

South African gold stocks are the exception. They pay large dividends and their shares are attractive in spite of the inherent risks resulting from the social unrest and turmoil associated with the country. If you want a high return, you also proportionally risk the capital you invested. Investors in Mexican stocks can attest to this.

Getting back to the discussion about the U.S. silver stocks—and the little ones in particular—this book will tend to concentrate on these because of the obviously greater opportunities inherent in them.

Almost all of the silver stocks in the U.S. are listed on the Spokane Stock Exchange or traded on that regional over-the-counter market. This exchange, started in 1897 and located in the then burgeoning city of Spokane, Washington, was the natural place for the silver stocks to be traded because the Coeur d'Alene Silver Mining Region was only 75 miles to the southeast in northern Idaho. This market expanded over the years; now almost 130 issues are traded on the Exchange and on that OTC regional market.

Even though silver is primarily a by-product of copper mining and half of all U.S. silver production comes as a result of copper mining, most of the remaining silver production comes from the mines in this world-famous district.

In 1981 almost 16 million ounces of silver were produced valued then at close to $240 million. Yes, these are not only the largest and the richest, but also the deepest silver mines in the U.S. This silver valley, which is only 20 miles long by 4 miles wide, is thought to be the most highly mineralized piece of real estate anywhere in the country.

How to Evaluate Them

If you were to invest in U.S. silver stocks, I would advise you to concentrate on those associated with the Coeur d'Alene Mining District. This is where the action is. It is *the* silver area, and the Spokane Stock Exchange is *the mecca for silver stocks.*

In making a decision on which of the smaller companies to go into, the investor should first get a solid background on silver. There are many excellent books on the subject including "Silver Profits In The 80's" by Jerome Smith and also several financial market letters of stature such as James Sibbet's "Let's Talk . . . Silver & Gold," Julian Snyder's "International Moneyline," Charles Stahl's "Green's Commodity Letter" and, of course, the "Silver and Gold Report" by Dan Rosenthal.

After getting a proper background, you will feel more confident and comfortable in investing in any particular industry. Certainly this goes for silver as well.

The silver stocks themselves are not difficult to understand. You will notice that most of them have a small number of shares outstanding, have funny sounding names and have properties or claims of varying sizes (refer to enclosed map).

Their claims are located alongside of, around and between those of the larger mining companies. Many of these smaller companies have been in existence for many years, but for numerous reasons their properties have not yet been put into production. This is due mostly to the fact that silver mining is expensive. Only those that had financial backing developed into major mines. Now, of course, all eyes are on the little companies with key holdings in the Coeur d'Alene Mining District because of the upturn in the price of silver.

The large oil companies and others are entering into joint ventures with the junior companies, and many are being merged into the giants.

So an investor should concentrate on the small silver mining stocks that have holdings favorably located near the big companies.

However, before you invest, it will help you to check your thinking with one of the knowledgeable brokers with one of the silver stock specialist firms.

How to Find Them and Follow the Quotes on Them

As pointed out earlier, the silver stocks are listed primarily on the Spokane Stock Exchange and/or traded on the regional OTC market. However, you will find some of the larger ones on the New York

Stock Exchange, the Pacific Coast Stock Exchange and on NASDAQ, and some are simultaneously on several markets.

The Wall Street Journal and *Barron's* do not publish silver stock prices other than those listed on the New York Stock Exchange. So the investor is forced to rely on his broker for quotes or on a newspaper from the Northwest.

The *Wallace Miner,* published weekly in Wallace, Idaho, covers all the silver stock prices. For the investor who has several silver stocks, it would be a good idea to subscribe to this publication. In general, however, the broker you use will be able to keep you informed on the prices.

How and When to Buy Them

If you intend to buy silver stocks, my advice would be to do so as quickly as possible. If silver goes to the heights expected by most experts, then prices of silver stocks today would have to be on the bargain counter.

It is all right to buy the larger silver stocks like Hecla Mining Company and Sunshine Mining Company through any of the New York Stock Exchange firms, but I would caution you to be careful on buying the smaller ones through them.

The New York Stock Exchange firms charge very high commissions on stocks under $2 per share. They also execute their orders through the New York OTC market makers who charge an additional markup for the execution. You can end up paying far more than the actual market by going this route.

The best way to buy the smaller silver stocks is through one of the specialist firms like National Securities Corporation in Seattle, Washington, or Pennaluna & Company in Spokane, Washington.

These firms will not only execute your orders in a reasonable and fair manner but also can help you to select the silver stocks that would be the most attractive at the time.

Keep in mind also that most of the "penny stocks" trade in 1000 share blocks and multiples thereof.

If you were going to invest $10,000 or less, I would perhaps limit diversification to maybe three issues. There is no sense in taking the "shotgun approach" as some would advise, spreading a small amount of money over a dozen stocks. It just complicates things and is unnecessary.

6

When to Sell Them

A transaction is never complete until a profit has been realized. How many times have we gone all the way up in price with a stock and all the way back down with it?

Selling a stock to realize a profit is extremely difficult for the average investor. It is important, therefore, to set some kind of margin of profit that you would be happy with at the time you buy it and then sell when it reaches that point.

Deciding when to sell the silver stocks will be unusually difficult because no one really knows how high and over what period of time silver will top out. All one can surmise is that the move will be big.

One way is to sell half of your position after a clear double in price and ride free with the balance.

Whatever you do after you buy—don't forget to take profits later.

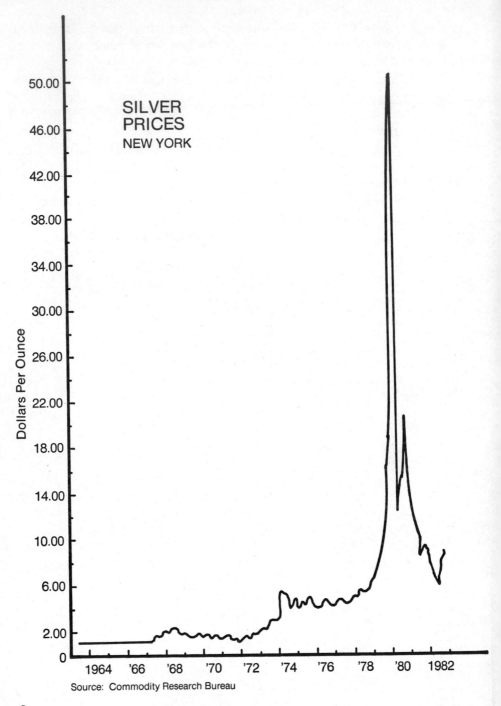

SILVER
PRICES
NEW YORK

Source: Commodity Research Bureau

8

3

A COMPENDIUM OF U.S. SILVER STOCKS

FOLLOWING is a brief summary of certain pertinent information on specific silver mining stocks. This does not purport to be a complete statement of all material facts concerning the securities properties described. These facts were obtained from reliable sources that are believed to be correct, but they are not guaranteed. The publication of this manual is not to be construed as a solicitation to buy or sell any stock mentioned herein.

Special Notes

The prices used for highs and lows on OTC stocks are the bid prices only. The bid price of a stock does not normally reflect an actual sale price, since many sales take place at the offer side of the market. Therefore, all the lows and highs were higher than indicated by varying amounts.

Also, many of the penny mining stocks that were involved with gold only have been arbitrarily left out of this study, since the purpose of this manual is to cover silver stocks primarily.

Aberdeen Idaho Mining Company

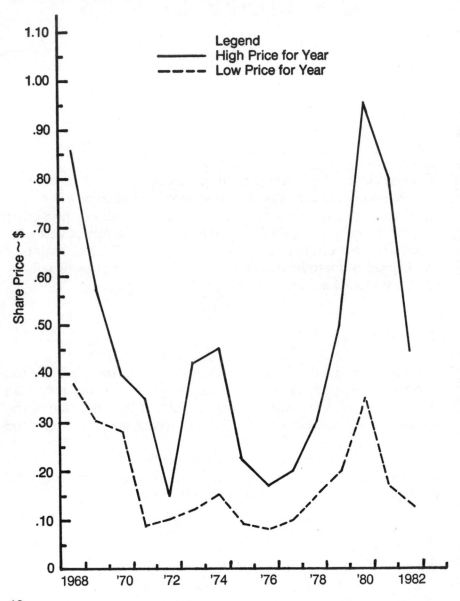

Spokane OTC
Inc. 1946
Idaho

P.O. Box 469
Wallace, ID 83873
Pres.–H.F. Magnuson
Sec.–D.L. Hess

Transfer Agent:
H.F. Magnuson & Co.
P.O. Box 469
Wallace, ID 83873

Aberdeen Idaho Mining Company

CAPITALIZATION:

One class of outstanding securities consisting of 3,000,000 shares of authorized nonassessable, capital stock with a par value of 10¢ per share. As of December 31, 1981, there were 2,274,612 shares issued and outstanding.

DESCRIPTION OF COMPANY:

The company's business consists of the ownership of mining claims located in Shoshone County, Idaho. The property of the company consists of 25 unpatented mining claims located in the Yreka Mining District. The company's property is subject to an operating agreement with the Bunker Hill division of Gulf Resources and Chemical Corp. At the present time, the company's property is not in production.

OPINION:

In view of the fact that the company's properties are located very strategically and the price has approached $1 in past active markets, I would look favorably on this stock.

PRICE HISTORY:

YEAR	HIGH	LOW
1968	.85	.38
1969	.57	.30
1970	.40	.28
1971	.35	.09
1972	.15	.10
1973	.42	.12
1974	.45	.15
1975	.22	.09
1976	.17	.08
1977	.20	.10
1978	.30	.15
1979	.50	.20
1980	.95	.35
1981	.80	.17
1982 to date	.46	.13

11

Abot
Mining
Company

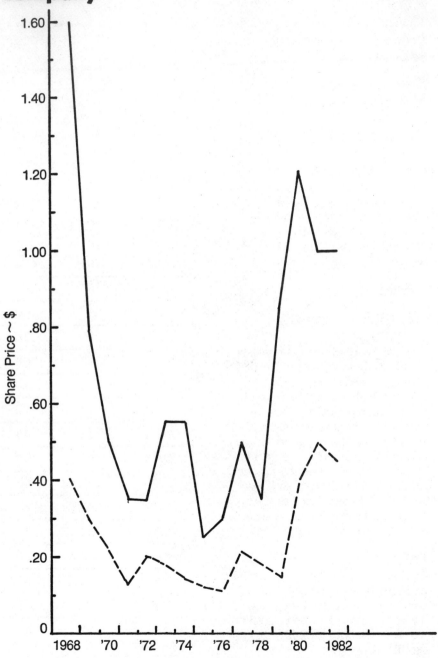

*Spokane OTC
Inc. 1957
Idaho*

Abot Mining Company

*P.O. Box 1010
Wallace, ID 83873
Pres.–Raymond H. Giles
Sec.–Dominic Peretti*

*Transfer Agent:
P.O. Box 1010
Wallace, ID 83873*

CAPITALIZATION:
10,000,000 shares authorized, par value 10¢; 5,885,719 shares issued and outstanding.

DESCRIPTION OF COMPANY:
Formed by Day Mines, Inc., to consolidate several mining properties north and east of DM's Gold Hunter mine. In 1968, part utilized with Gold Hunter and eastern portion of Independence Lead. Remainder utilized with claims owned by Hecla Mining and leased to it. Hecla subsequently drove long exploratory crosscut from 4,050-foot level of its Lucky Friday mine, but North Abot area not yet reached.

OPINION:
Abot is one of the most attractive of the junior silver mining stocks in the CDA Silver Mining District. Hecla's acquisition of 42% of the stock would indicate that in all probability they will acquire the balance of it. Would include this stock in any portfolio of the smaller companies.

PRICE HISTORY:

YEAR	HIGH	LOW
1968	1.60	.40
1969	.80	.30
1970	.50	.22
1971	.35	.13
1972	.35	.20
1973	.55	.18
1974	.55	.14
1975	.25	.12
1976	.30	.11
1977	.50	.21
1978	.35	.18
1979	.85	.15
1980	1.20	.40
1981	1.00	.50
1982 to date	1.00	.45

13

Admiral Consolidated Mining Company

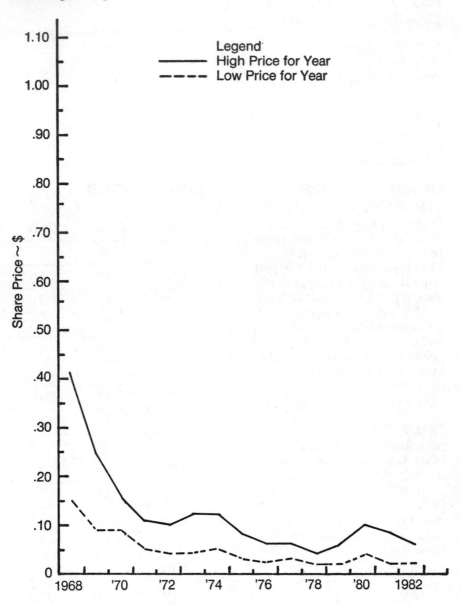

*Spokane OTC
Inc. 1921
Idaho*

*P.O. Box 487
Portland, OR 97207*

*Pres.–Karl W. Jasper
Sec.–M.W. Onstine*

*Transfer Agent:
Burton W. Onstine
P.O. Box 487
Portland, OR 97207*

Admiral Consolidated Mining Company

CAPITALIZATION:
4,000,000 shares authorized, par value 10¢; 2,541,019 shares of common stock outstanding.

DESCRIPTION OF COMPANY:
Holds four state leases totaling 360 acres near Leadpoint, Stevens County, Washington, astride the Metaline limestone. The Admiral mine yielded some direct-shipping zinc ore and 765 tons of mill concentrates years ago. Only assessment work being done now. Firm also has mineral rights on 560 acres near old Cleveland mine in southwestern Stevens County.

OPINION:
None.

PRICE HISTORY:

YEAR	HIGH	LOW
1968	.41	.15
1969	.25	.09
1970	.16	.09
1971	.11	.05
1972	.10	.04
1973	.12	.04
1974	.12	.05
1975	.08	.03
1976	.06	.02
1977	.06	.03
1978	.04	.02
1979	.06	.02
1980	.10	.04
1981	.08	.02
1982 to date	.06	.02

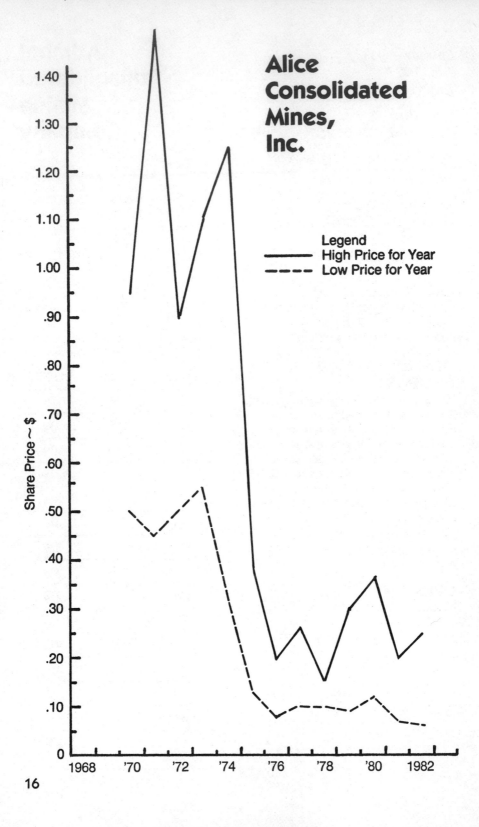

Alice
Consolidated
Mines,
Inc.

Legend
——— High Price for Year
- - - - Low Price for Year

Share Price ~ $

1.40
1.30
1.20
1.10
1.00
.90
.80
.70
.60
.50
.40
.30
.20
.10
0

1968   '70   '72   '74   '76   '78   '80   1982

16

*Spokane OTC
Inc. 1969 Idaho*

*P.O. Box 469
Wallace, ID 83873*

*Pres. – Wray Featherstone
Sec. – D.L. Hess*

*Transfer Agent:
H.F. Magnuson & Co.
P.O. Box 469
Wallace, ID 83873*

Alice Consolidated Mines, Inc.

CAPITALIZATION:
One class of outstanding securities consisting of 10,000,000 shares of authorized nonassessable, capital stock with a par value of 10¢ per share. As of December 31, 1981, there were 8,029,675 shares of stock issued and outstanding.

DESCRIPTION OF COMPANY:
Incorporated to consolidate 1,169 acres of mineral properties in the southeast portion of the Golconda Area, Hunter Mining District, Shoshone County, Idaho. The consolidated area included all the properties held by Mullan Silver-Lead Company, United Lead-Zinc Mines Company, Alice Silver-Lead Mining Company and also smaller areas owned by Golconda Mining Corp. and Square Deal Mining & Milling Co. Golconda owns approximately 54% of the outstanding shares of Alice Consolidated.

OPINION:
Would only be attractive on the basis of a major move in silver.

PRICE HISTORY:

YEAR	HIGH	LOW
1970	.95	.50
1971	1.50	.45
1972	.90	.50
1973	1.10	.55
1974	1.25	.30
1975	.38	.13
1976	.20	.08
1977	.26	.10
1978	.15	.10
1979	.30	.09
1980	.36	.12
1981	.20	.07
1982 to date	.25	.06

Allied
Silver
Lead
Company

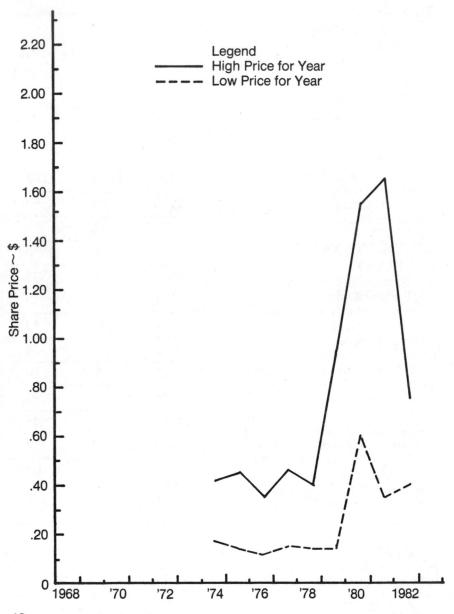

*Spokane Stock Exchange
Inc. 1967
Idaho*

*P.O. Box 463
Mullan, Idaho 83846*
Pres. – Elmer Almquist
Sec. – D.G. McClary

Transfer Agent:
P.O. Box 463
Mullan, ID 83846

Allied Silver Lead Company

CAPITALIZATION:
Authorized 1,000,000 shares of
10¢ par value each. On May 7,
1968, the common, nonassessable shares were increased to
5,000,000 with a par value of 2¢
each. In 1974 a five-for-one
stock split increased the outstanding capital stock from
622,761 shares to 3,113,804
shares; 3,171,625 shares outstanding.

DESCRIPTION OF COMPANY:
Acquired subsurface mineral
rights to 99% of Mullan, Idaho,
totaling 416 acres. Shares issued
to owners of lots and city-owned
property leased. In 1981 leased
mineral rights holdings north of
Osburn fault to Sunshine Mining
Co. That firm has been doing
downhole drilling to probe
western extension of Lucky
Friday mine vein zone.

OPINION:
One of the better quality penny
silver stocks that has above
average prospects.

PRICE HISTORY:

YEAR	HIGH	LOW
1974	.42	.17
1975	.45	.14
1976	.35	.12
1977	.46	.15
1978	.40	.14
1979	95	.14
1980	1.55	.60
1981	1.65	.35
1982 to date	.75	.40

Amazon Dixie Mining Company

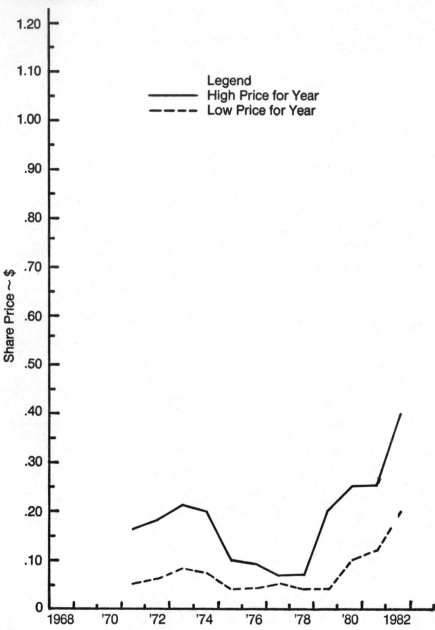

Spokane OTC
Inc. 1966
Idaho

P.O. Box 469
Wallace, ID 83873
Pres.–H.F. Magnuson
Sec.–D.L. Hess

Transfer Agent:
H.F. Magnuson
P.O. Box 469
Wallace, ID 83873

Amazon Dixie Mining Company

CAPITALIZATION:
Authorized 3,000,000 shares of nonassessable, capital stock with a par value of 10¢ per share. As of December 31, 1981, there were 2,343,195 shares of stock issued and outstanding.

DESCRIPTION OF COMPANY:
Owns 11 patented and 32 unpatented claims east of Mullan and across Idaho border in Mineral County, Montana. Old workings include an 800-foot tunnel. In September, 1982, announcement made that Bear Creek Mining Co., a division of Kennecott Corp., had leased the claims and then assigned them to Anaconda Minerals Co., a division of Atlantic Richfield Co., for exploration.

OPINION:
Because of the joint venture with Atlantic Richfield, the stock has become one of the more attractive issues.

PRICE HISTORY:

YEAR	HIGH	LOW
1971	.16	.05
1972	.18	.06
1973	.21	.08
1974	.20	.07
1975	.10	.04
1976	.09	.04
1977	.07	.05
1978	.07	.04
1979	.20	.04
1980	.25	.10
1981	.25	.12
1982 to date	.40	.20

21

American
Silver
Mining
Company

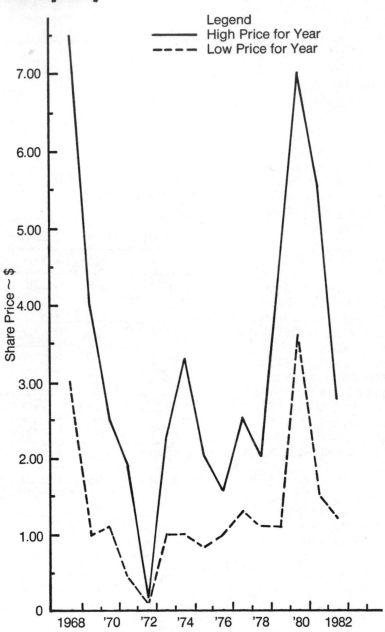

Legend
——— High Price for Year
- - - - Low Price for Year

Share Price ~ $

7.00

6.00

5.00

4.00

3.00

2.00

1.00

0

1968 '70 '72 '74 '76 '78 '80 1982

Spokane OTC
Inc. 1924
Idaho

East 2503 17th Ave.
Spokane, WA 99203
Pres.–E. Wofford Conrad
Sec.–Enid Conrad

Transfer Agent:
East 2503 1th Ave.
Spokane, WA 99203

American Silver Mining Company

CAPITALIZATION:
Authorized capital, 3,000,000 shares, par value 10¢ each. Shares outstanding, 2,566,000 with approximately 2,000 shareholders.

DESCRIPTION OF COMPANY:
Property consists of 20 un-patented mining claims, some fractions, located in Idaho's Coeur d'Alene Mining District. The property is surrounded on three sides by mining claims owned by Coeur d'Alene Mines Corp. and workings of the latter's old Mineral Point mine extend into American Silver on the north. The new Coeur mine is to the east. On the west is ground held by Merger Mines and included in Coeur d'Alene Mines' CAMP exploration project. On June 25, 1980, shareholders ratified an agreement with ASARCO and Coeur d'Alene Mines under which the American Silver property and two properties south of it acquired by Coeur d'Alene Mines were divided into four lease blocks for exploration and development.

PRICE HISTORY:

YEAR	HIGH	LOW
1968	7.50	3.00
1969	4.00	1.00
1970	2.50	1.10
1971	1.90	.40
1972	.18	.06
1973	2.25	1.00
1974	3.25	1.00
1975	2.00	.85
1976	1.60	1.00
1977	2.50	1.30
1978	2.00	1.10
1979	5.00	1.10
1980	7.00	3.60
1981	5.50	1.50
1982 to date	2.75	1.20

OPINION:
One of the higher quality junior silver mining companies; is also a merger candidate and with higher silver prices, as it has done in the past, could sell for substantially more than its current market price.

23

ASARCO, Inc.

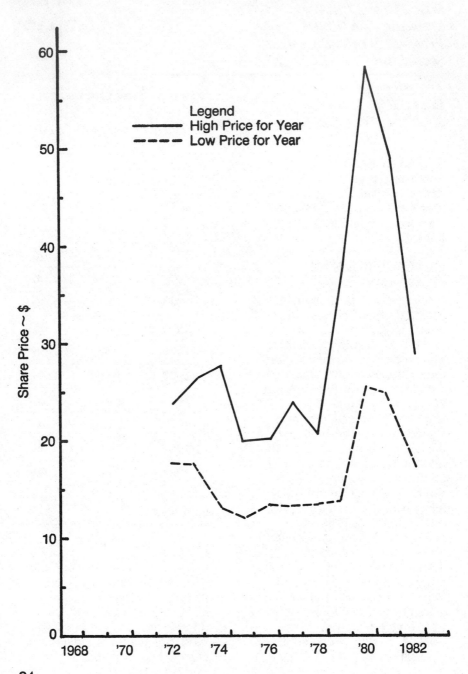

New York Stock Exchange
Inc. 1899
New Jersey

ASARCO, Inc.

120 Broadway
New York, NY 10271
(212) 669-1000
Pres.–R. deJ. Osborne
Sec.–A.J. Gillespie, Jr.

Transfer Agent:
Morgan Guaranty Trust
 Co.
30 W. Broadway
New York, NY 10015

CAPITALIZATION:
Authorized common stock,
23,663,252 shares (no par); preferred stock ($7 & $6.25),
1,550,000 and 1,250 shares, the
latter convertible into 0.8381
common.

DESCRIPTION OF COMPANY:
AR is a major producer of silver,
copper, lead and zinc and holds
sizable interests in foreign
mining concerns. Silver production in 1981 equaled 10,343,000
ounces.

OPINION:
ASARCO is looked upon as a
silver stock even though it pro-
duces many other metals. The
stock appears cheap, and price
could work higher on higher
silver and copper prices.

PRICE HISTORY:

YEAR	HIGH	LOW
1972	23½	17½
1973	26⅛	17¼
1974	27⅜	13
1975	19¾	12
1976	20	13⅛
1977	23⅝	13
1978	20⅜	13¼
1979	37⅞	13⅝
1980	58½	25½
1981	48½	24¾
1982 to date	38¾	17¼

Atlas Mining Company

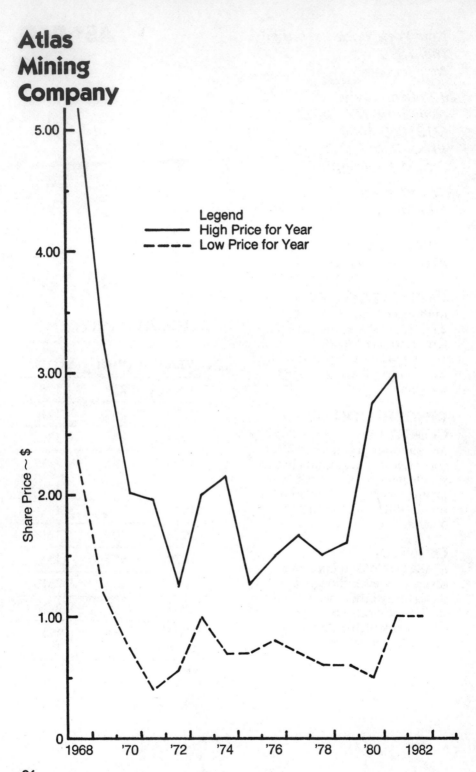

Legend
High Price for Year
Low Price for Year

Spokane OTC
Inc. 1924
Idaho

P.O. Box 1088
Wallace, ID 83873
Pres.–John S. Pehar
Sec.–Thomas E. Groce

Transfer Agent:
P.O. Box 1088
Wallace, ID 83873

Atlas Mining Company

CAPITALIZATION:
Authorized capital, 5,000,000 shares, par value 10¢. Issued and outstanding shares, 2,412,500.

DESCRIPTION OF COMPANY:
A consolidation of half a dozen prospects, the Atlas property consists of 31 patented and 30 unpatented claims and some fee ground south of Hecla's Lucky Friday mine. Most recent development work done by Noranda Exploration, Inc., 1973–1977. Under a 1982 agreement settling litigation with Hecla over extra-lateral rights to ore being mined in Lucky Friday, Hecla is paying Atlas $200,000 for 38 acres of disputed land and undertaking a three-year, $1.3 million exploration project from the long Atlas Tunnel. Principal shareholders: Bache, Halsey, Stuart & Shields now own 177,170 shares of stock being 6.855% of the outstanding shares. Other large blocks of stock are owned by private parties.

OPINION:
Would have to be rated as a buy.

PRICE HISTORY:

YEAR	HIGH	LOW
1968	5.25	2.25
1969	3.25	1.20
1970	2.00	.75
1971	1.95	.40
1972	1.25	.55
1973	2.00	1.00
1974	2.15	.70
1975	1.25	.70
1976	1.50	.80
1977	1.65	.70
1978	1.50	.60
1979	1.60	.60
1980	2.75	.50
1981	3.00	1.00
1982 to date	1.50	1.00

Beacon
Light
Mining
Company

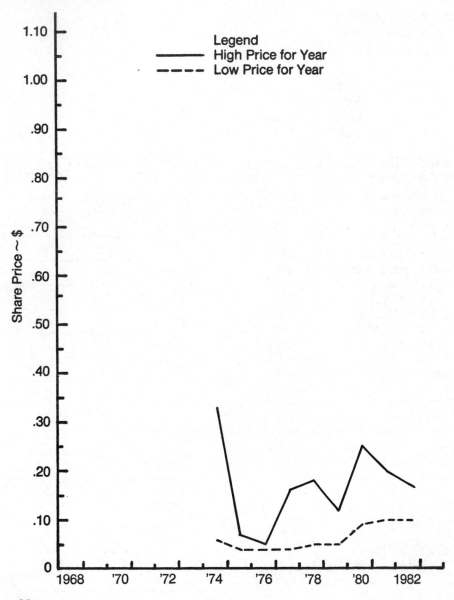

Spokane OTC
Inc. 1953
Idaho

P.O. Box 969
Wallace, ID 83873
Pres. – George R. DeNise
Sec. – Marjorie Rieske

Beacon Light Mining Company

Transfer Agent:
Majorie Rieske
609 Bank St.
Wallace, ID 83873

CAPITALIZATION:
Authorized 10,000,000 shares, par value 10¢. Issued and outstanding, 3,038,141 shares.

DESCRIPTION OF COMPANY:
76 unpatented mining claims. Three adits, approximately 5,000 feet of tunnel. Mineralization silver, lead and copper. Located east of Idaho Silver and south of Princeton along U.S. Highway 10, mostly in Idaho, but covering Lookout Pass.

OPINION:
Fully priced right now, but could move high on a huge move in the price of silver.

PRICE HISTORY:

YEAR	HIGH	LOW
1974	.33	.06
1975	.07	.04
1976	.05	.04
1977	.16	.04
1978	.18	.05
1979	.12	.05
1980	.25	.09
1981	.20	.10
1982 to date	.17	.10

29

Bismarck
Mining
Company

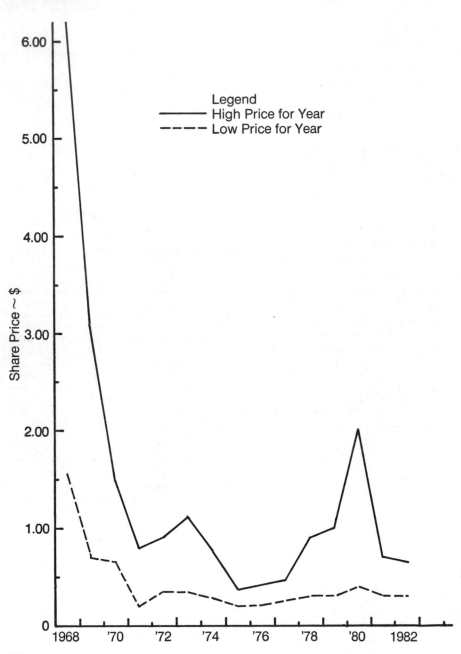

Spokane OTC
Inc. 1924
Idaho

Bismarck Mining Company

P.O. Box 1080
Kellogg, ID 83873
Pres.—Piatt Hull
Sec.—Ronald Eggert

Transfer Agent:
H.F. Magnuson & Co.
P.O. Box 469
Wallace, ID 83873

CAPITALIZATION:
Authorized 1,500,000 shares,
10¢ par value; 1,500,000 shares
issued and outstanding.

DESCRIPTION OF COMPANY:
Holds 48 claims in Big Creek
area of CDA District Silver Belt.
Control held by Sunshine, which
drove mile-long exploratory
tunnel to Bismarck vein from
2,700-foot level of Sun Con area
of Sunshine mine. Work suspended in 1971 pending sinking
of No. 12 Sunshine shaft to give
deeper access to the area.

OPINION:
The completion of the No. 12
shaft and the opening up of the
surrounding properties should
give quite a price boost to stocks
like Bismarck. Also would have
to be considered a takeover candidate.

PRICE HISTORY:

YEAR	HIGH	LOW
1968	6.25	1.55
1969	3.10	.70
1970	1.50	.65
1971	.80	.20
1972	.90	.35
1973	1.10	.35
1974	.75	.27
1975	.38	.20
1976	.43	.21
1977	.47	.26
1978	.90	.30
1979	1.00	.30
1980	2.00	.40
1981	.70	.30
1982 to date	.65	.30

Bonanza
Gold,
Inc.

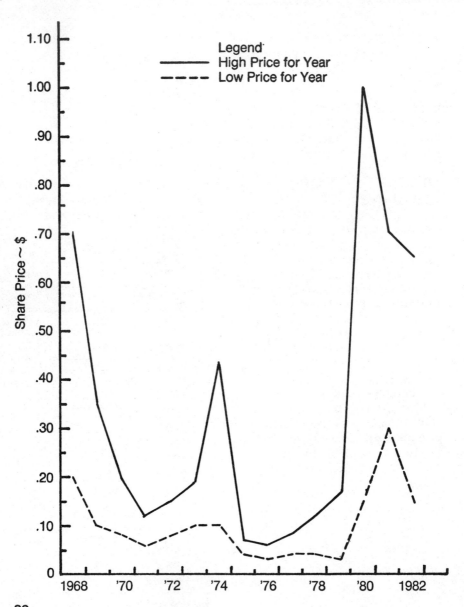

Spokane OTC
Inc. 1961
Idaho

505 Northtown Office
  Bldg.
Spokane, WA 99207
Pres. –Robert Kistler
Sec. –Hobart Teneff

Transfer Agent:
505 Northtown Office
  Bldg.
Spokane, WA 99207

Bonanza Gold, Inc.

CAPITALIZATION:
Authorized 6,000,000 shares;
2,986,800 issued and outstanding.

DESCRIPTION OF COMPANY:
Holds 22 claims just north of Osburn and 56 claims 6 miles south of Kellogg, both in CDA District. Company drilled three test holes at its Osburn property in 1970 which were said to have intercepted silver mineralization. In 1973 acquired an eight claim gold prospect near Butte, Montana. Owns 174,759 shares of Capitol Silver Mines, Inc. and 5,225 shares of Judith Gold Corp.

OPINION:
Stock is near its old highs, however could move up with an increase in silver prices.

PRICE HISTORY:

YEAR	HIGH	LOW
1968	.70	.20
1969	.35	.10
1970	.20	.08
1971	.12	.06
1972	.15	.08
1973	.19	.10
1974	.43	.10
1975	.07	.04
1976	.06	.03
1977	.08	.04
1978	.12	.04
1979	.17	.03
1980	1.00	.15
1981	.70	.30
1982 to date	.65	.15

33

Bullion
Lode
Silver
Mining
Company

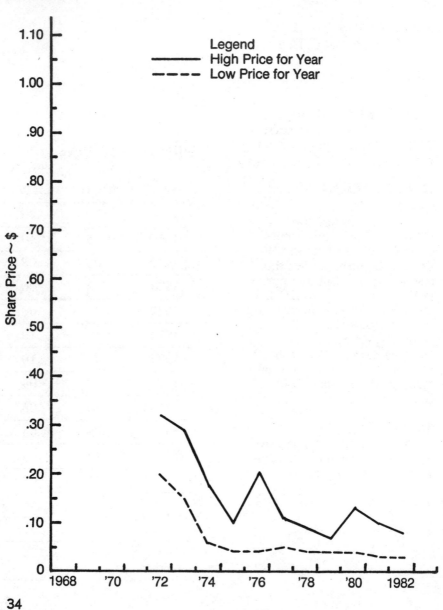

*Spokane OTC
Inc. 1968
Idaho*

*1710 East Trent Ave.
Spokane, WA 99201
Pres.—Bruce Parsons
Sec.—Joseph R. Edington*

*Transfer Agent:
Spokane Guaranty Co.
1306 Washington Mutual
   Bldg.
Spokane, WA 99201*

CAPITALIZATION:
Authorized 5,000,000 shares of common no par value stock; 2,098,200 shares issued and outstanding.

DESCRIPTION OF COMPANY:
The property held consists of one patented and 10 unpatented mining claims located in the Florence Mining District of Idaho. Some crude silver-gold ore reportedly shipped in 1971 and 1973. Monogram Development, Limited, which had a lease to the claims, terminated the lease in September, 1981, due to low price of metals. Claims are not being explored at this time.

OPINION:
None.

PRICE HISTORY:

YEAR	HIGH	LOW
1972	.32	.20
1973	.29	.15
1974	.18	.06
1975	.10	.04
1976	.20	.04
1977	.11	.05
1978	.09	.04
1979	.07	.04
1980	.13	.04
1981	.10	.03
1982 to date	.08	.03

Bunker
Chance
Mining
Company

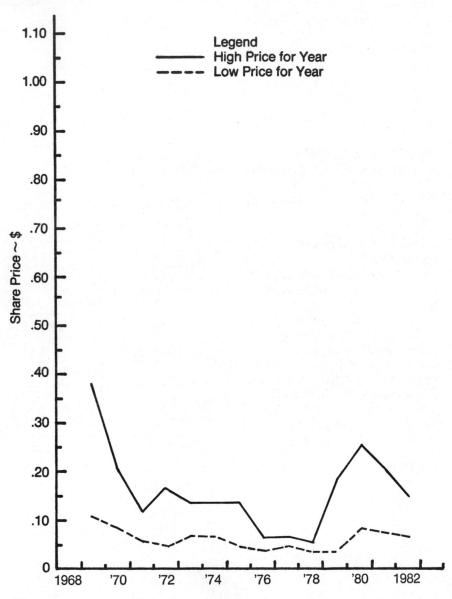

Bunker Chance Mining Company

Spokane OTC
Inc. 1922
Idaho

P.O. Box 605
Smelterville, ID 83868
Pres. – Daniel Davidoff
Sec./Treas. – Oliver W.
Silfvast

Transfer Agent:
P.O. Box 605
Smelterville, ID 83868

CAPITALIZATION:
Authorized 6,000,000 shares of
the par value of 5¢ per share.

DESCRIPTION OF COMPANY:
Holds eight-claim property abutting the town of Wardner, Idaho, and claims of Bunker Hill and Yreka United. Some exploration of property done by Bunker Hill from its mine workings. Only annual assessment work now being performed.

OPINION:
When a deal is made and if Bunker Hill gets back into production, Bunker Chance could come to life.

PRICE HISTORY:

YEAR	HIGH	LOW
1969	.37	.10
1970	.20	.08
1971	.11	.05
1972	.16	.04
1973	.13	.06
1974	.13	.06
1975	.13	.04
1976	.06	.03
1977	.06	.04
1978	.05	.03
1979	.18	.03
1980	.25	.08
1981	.20	.07
1982 to date	.14	.06

Burke
Mining
Company

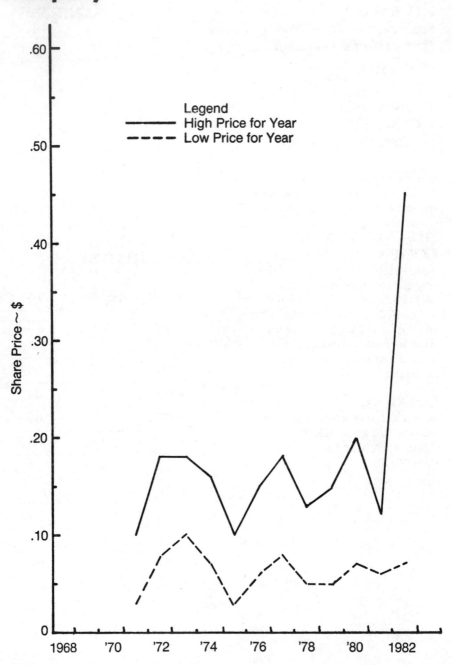

Spokane OTC
Inc. 1967
Idaho

P.O. Box 469
Wallace, ID 83873
Pres. – Walter L. Sly
Sec. – R.M. MacPhee

Transfer Agent:
P.O. Box 469
Wallace, ID 83873

Burke Mining Company

CAPITALIZATION:
One class outstanding securities consisting of 6,000,000 shares of authorized nonassessable capital stock with a par value of 10¢ per share; 5,301,797 shares issued and outstanding.

DESCRIPTION OF COMPANY:
Owns 200 claims in northeastern sector of CDA District. Burke recently was leased to Pacific Coast Mines, a subsidiary of U.S. Borax & Chemical Corporation. The lessee already is doing test drilling, and the area is said to contain strata-bound copper deposits.

OPINION:
Because of the location of its properties in relationship to some of the larger mines and in view of the recent joint venture with U.S. Borax, Burke would have to be considered a buy.

PRICE HISTORY:

YEAR	HIGH	LOW
1971	.10	.03
1972	.18	.08
1973	.18	.10
1974	.16	.07
1975	.10	.03
1976	.15	.06
1977	.18	.08
1978	.13	.05
1979	.15	.05
1980	.20	.07
1981	.12	.06
1982 to date	.45	.07

Caledonia
Silver
Lead
Mines,
Company

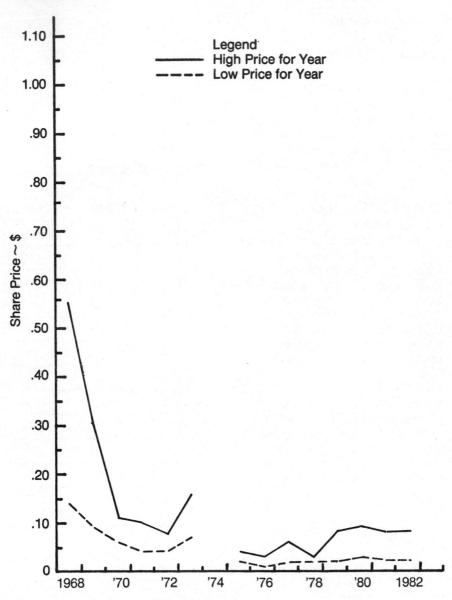

Spokane OTC
Inc. 1927
Idaho

504½ Bank St.
Wallace, ID 83873
Pres.—Frank Morbeck
Sec./Treas.—Virginia
Mattern

Transfer Agent:
504½ Bank St.
P.O. Box 1127
Wallace, ID 83873

Caledonia Silver Lead Mines, Company

CAPITALIZATION:
Authorized 5,000,000 shares,
par value 10¢; 4,975,097 shares
issued and outstanding.

DESCRIPTION OF COMPANY:
Owns 14 unpatented claims in
western Montana adjoining the
Tarbox mine, 12 unpatented
mining claims, Nordic Group, on
Coal Creek in Shoshone County,
Idaho. The company anticipates
doing their annual assessment
work on their properties as well
as some geological and development work.

OPINION:
One of the many silver stocks
that could move up if silver has a
major move upward from its
present point.

PRICE HISTORY:

YEAR	HIGH	LOW
1968	.55	.14
1969	.30	.09
1970	.11	.06
1971	.10	.04
1972	.08	.04
1973	.16	.07
1974		
1975	.04	.02
1976	.03	.01
1977	.06	.02
1978	.03	.02
1979	.08	.02
1980	.09	.03
1981	.08	.02
1982 to date	.08	.02

41

Callahan Consolidated Mines, Inc.

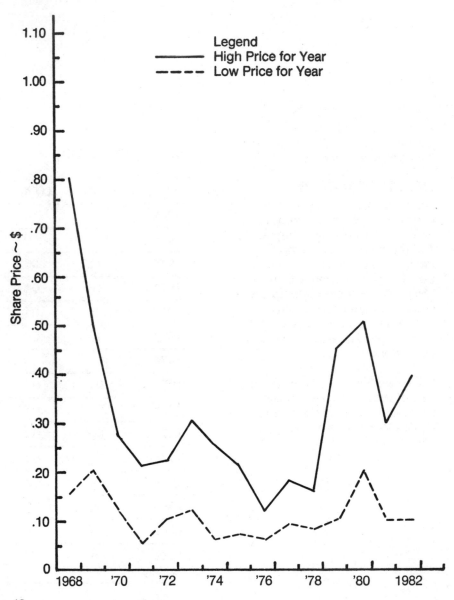

42

Spokane OTC
Inc. 1937
Idaho

P.O. Box 469
Wallace, ID 83873
Pres. – George M. Grismer
Sec. – D.L. Hess

Transfer Agent:
H.F. Magnuson & Co.
P.O. Box 469
Wallace, ID 83873

Callahan Consolidated Mines, Inc.

CAPITALIZATION:

Authorized 3,500,000 shares of capital stock with a par value of 10¢ per share. As of December 31, 1981, there were 3,499,964 shares of stock issued and outstanding.

DESCRIPTION OF COMPANY:

Owns Temple group of five patented claims and half interest in Sabina patented claims in Burke, Idaho, area. Neither being worked. Has substantial assets through ownership of the following shares of other mining companies: 10,000 shares of Abot Mining, 8,100 shares of American Silver, and 88,690 shares of Coeur d'Alene Mines.

OPINION:

Callahan Consolidated is always one of the attractive stocks when silver is advancing.

PRICE HISTORY:

YEAR	HIGH	LOW
1968	.80	.15
1969	.50	.20
1970	.27	.12
1971	.21	.05
1972	.22	.10
1973	.30	.12
1974	.25	.06
1975	.21	.07
1976	.12	.06
1977	.18	.09
1978	.16	.08
1979	.45	.10
1980	.50	.20
1981	.30	.10
1982 to date	.39	.10

Callahan
Mining
Company

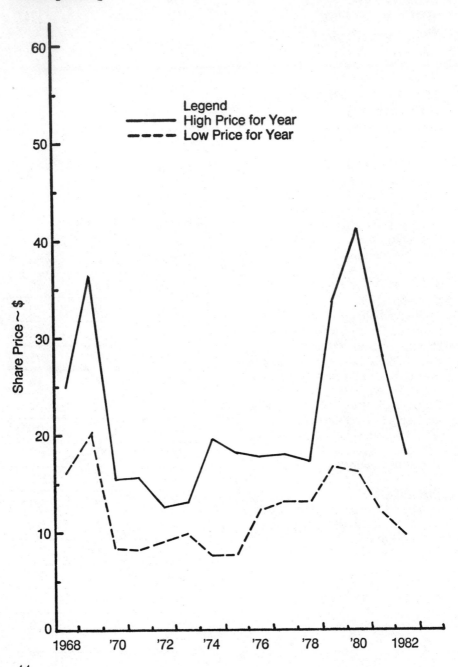

New York Stock Exchange
Spokane Stock Exchange
Inc. 1912
Arizona

6245 North 24th St.
Phoenix, AZ 85016
Pres. – Charles D. Snead

Transfer Agent:
Bank of New York
90 Washington St.
New York, NY 10015

Callahan Mining Company

CAPITALIZATION:
Common stock: 6,279,939 ($1 par) outstanding.

DESCRIPTION OF COMPANY:
Owns Idaho Galena mine property just west of Wallace. Receives 50% of cash flow from the ASARCO-operated Galena mine which ranks as second largest U.S. silver producer. 1981 output was 3,501,652 troy ounces. Callahan also receives 5% of profits from adjoining ASARCO-operated Coeur mine which ranked No. 3 in 1981 with 2,598,710 ounces of silver. Callahan is sinking a 5,100-foot shaft at Caladay property just east of the Galena property in a $26.6 million exploration project. Also funding up to 8% of ASARCO's $3.5 million American Silver Project just west of Coeur mine.

OPINION:
One of the well-known listed silver stocks that belongs in every large portfolio.

PRICE HISTORY:

YEAR	HIGH	LOW
1968	24.75	16.00
1969	36.50	20.00
1970	15.25	8.30
1971	15.50	8.25
1972	12.50	9.00
1973	13.00	9.75
1974	19.50	7.50
1975	18.00	7.50
1976	17.50	12.00
1977	17.75	13.00
1978	17.00	13.00
1979	33.50	16.50
1980	41.00	16.00
1981	28.00	11.75
1982 to date	17.75	9.50

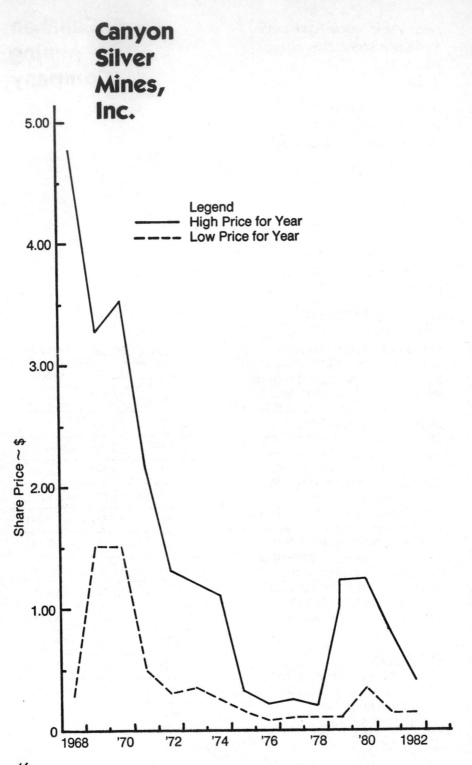

Canyon Silver Mines, Inc.

Share Price ~ $

Legend
——— High Price for Year
----- Low Price for Year

Spokane OTC
Inc. 1965
Idaho

Osburn, ID 83849
Pres. — Iris Morrow
Sec. — S.L. Anderson

Transfer Agent:
P.O. Box 746
Osburn, ID 83849

Canyon Silver Mines, Inc.

CAPITALIZATION:
Authorized 5,000,000 shares; 3,304,660 shares issued and outstanding.

DESCRIPTION OF COMPANY:
Owns old Formosa mine property 2 miles up road from Wallace to Burke, Idaho. Company reopened main adit in 1965, deepened shaft and developed some lead-silver ore before various problems caused suspension of operation.

OPINION:
Higher silver prices will cause considerable interest in Canyon stock again.

PRICE HISTORY:

YEAR	HIGH	LOW
1968	4.75	.30
1969	3.25	1.50
1970	3.50	1.50
1971	2.15	.50
1972	1.30	.30
1973	1.20	.35
1974	1.10	.25
1975	.32	.15
1976	.21	.08
1977	.26	.10
1978	.19	.10
1979	1.20	.10
1980	1.20	.35
1981	.85	.15
1982 to date	.40	.14

Capitol Silver Mines, Inc.

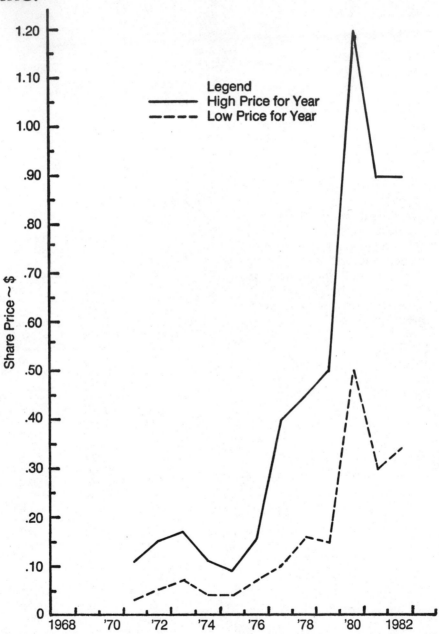

Share Price ~ $

Legend
— High Price for Year
--- Low Price for Year

*Spokane OTC
Inc. 1967
Idaho*

*P.O. Box 469
Wallace, ID 83873
Pres. – Walter L. Sly
Sec. – R.M. MacPhee*

*Transfer Agent:
H.F. Magnuson & Co.
P.O. Box 469
Wallace, ID 83873*

Capitol Silver Mines, Inc.

CAPITALIZATION:

Authorized capital of 6,000,000 shares of 10¢ par value stock of which 5,560,833 shares are issued and outstanding as of December 31, 1981.

DESCRIPTION OF COMPANY:

Staked more than 288 claims north of Osburn, CDA District. The claims lay between the Royal-Apex and Highland Aurora properties which Bunker Hill Co. had undertaken to develop.

OPINION:

One of the more attractive silver stocks in the CDA Mining Region that offers unusual potential.

PRICE HISTORY:

YEAR	HIGH	LOW
1971	.11	.03
1972	.15	.05
1973	.17	.07
1974	.11	.04
1975	.09	.04
1976	.16	.07
1977	.40	.10
1978	.45	.16
1979	.50	.15
1980	1.20	.50
1981	.90	.30
1982 to date	.90	.34

Century Silver Mines, Inc.

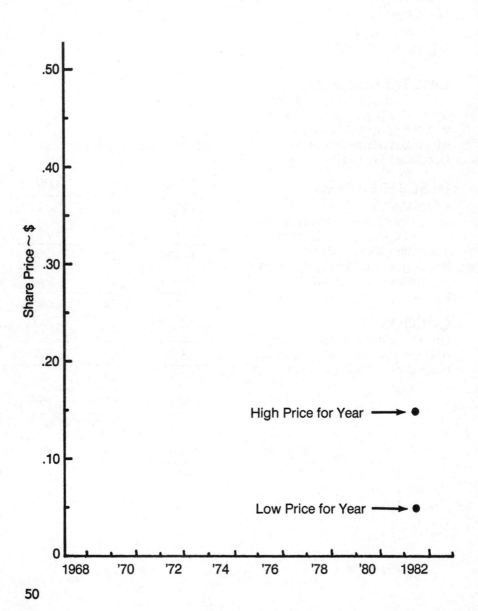

Share Price ~ $

High Price for Year ⟶ ●

Low Price for Year ⟶ ●

1968   '70   '72   '74   '76   '78   '80   1982

Idaho First National
  Bank Bldg.
Wallace, ID 83873
Pres. –Dr. John G. Branz
Sec./Treas. –Jack E. Scott

Transfer Agent:
P.O. Box 1088
Wallace, ID 83873

Century Silver Mines, Inc.

CAPITALIZATION:
Common stock, nonassessable, par value 10¢ per share, authorized 10,000,000 shares, issued and outstanding 1,592,492 shares.

DESCRIPTION OF COMPANY:
Acquired interests in 11 patented and 14 unpatented claims near Rimini, Montana, southwest of Helena; opened old workings and confirmed silver-gold-lead-zinc values shown on old maps. Sparrow Resources, Calgary, entered into purchase agreement in 1974, and in 1981 a consulting firm estimated ore reserves at more than 500,000 tons. Century obtained court order of default in May, 1982.

OPINION:
None.

PRICE HISTORY:

YEAR	HIGH	LOW
1982	.15	.05

Champion Gold and Silver, Inc.

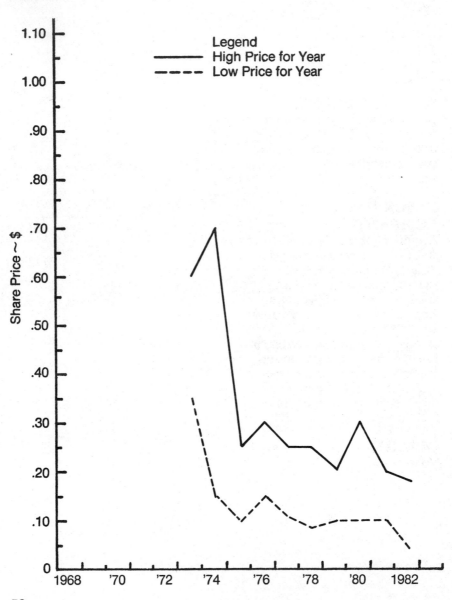

Legend
——— High Price for Year
- - - - Low Price for Year

Share Price ~ $

1.10
1.00
.90
.80
.70
.60
.50
.40
.30
.20
.10
0

1968   '70   '72   '74   '76   '78   '80   1982

Spokane OTC
Inc. 1967
Idaho

P.O. Box 488
11 N. 2nd St., Suite 202
Coeur d'Alene, ID 83814
Pres.–Peter W. Laczay
Sec.–M.J. Butcher

Transfer Agent:
Spokane Guaranty Co.
1306 Washington Mutual
*   Bank Bldg.*
Spokane, WA 99201

Champion Gold and Silver, Inc.

CAPITALIZATION:

Authorized 5,000,000 shares of 10¢ par value common non-assessable stock; 4,627,219 shares issued and outstanding with approximately 200 share-holders.

DESCRIPTION OF COMPANY:

Exploratory drilling of its First Thought gold property of three patented claims near Orient, Washington, started in August, 1982, by Shell Oil under 75/25 operating agreement calling for minimum expenditure of $120,000 over first three years. Pacific Coast Mines (U.S. Borax subsidiary) in 1982 leased all 226 Champion claims in Burke, Idaho, area under 75/25 operating agreement providing for minimum expenditure of $200,000 over first four years. Company mill testing gold-silver ore at its Silver Bell mine, Clancy, Montana.

PRICE HISTORY:

YEAR	HIGH	LOW
1973	.60	.35
1974	.70	.15
1975	.25	.10
1976	.30	.15
1977	.25	.11
1978	.25	.08
1979	.21	.10
1980	.30	.10
1981	.20	.10
1982 to date	.18	.04

OPINION:

Could be attractive on the basis of a joint venture with U.S. Borax.

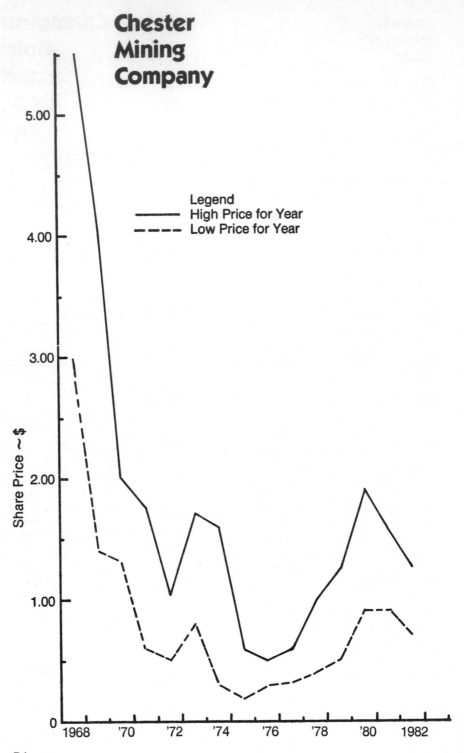

Chester Mining Company

Legend
—— High Price for Year
- - - Low Price for Year

Share Price ~ $

5.00

4.00

3.00

2.00

1.00

0

1968   '70   '72   '74   '76   '78   '80   1982

Spokane OTC
Inc. 1900
Idaho

P.O. Box 320
Wallace, ID 83873
Pres. – William A. Griffith
Sec. – D.W. Morehouse

Transfer Agent:
P.O. Box 320
Wallace, ID 83873

Chester Mining Company

CAPITALIZATION:
Authorized 1,000,000 shares of common capital stock of the par value 2½¢, of which 916,645 shares are issued and outstanding.

DESCRIPTION OF COMPANY:
Chester Mining Company receives royalties from its "Chester Area" which is leased to the Unit Area operators (Sunshine Mining Co., Hecla Mining Co.). The Chester Area is a 200-foot-wide strip on each side of Chester's vein and consists of approximately 12 acres. In addition to the Chester Area, Chester Mining Company owns an undivided one-third interest in any and all ore within the "Mineral Mountain Area." Hecla Mining Co. is the owner of 496,796 shares, or 54.20% of the total shares outstanding.

OPINION:
Chester has a very small capitalization and is closely held; with higher silver prices the stock could be very attractive.

PRICE HISTORY:

YEAR	HIGH	LOW
1968	5.50	3.00
1969	4.00	1.40
1970	2.00	1.25
1971	1.75	.60
1972	1.10	.50
1973	1.70	.80
1974	1.60	.30
1975	.60	.20
1976	.50	.30
1977	.60	.31
1978	1.00	.40
1979	1.25	.50
1980	1.90	.90
1981	1.60	.90
1982 to date	1.25	.70

55

Clayton Silver Mines, Inc.

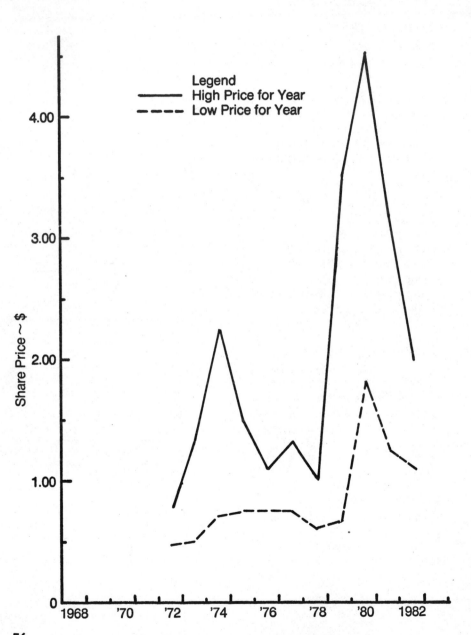

Spokane Stock Exchange
Pacific Stock Exchange
Inc. 1934
Arizona

P.O. Box 469
Wallace, ID 83873
Pres. –H.F. Magnuson

Transfer Agent:
Seattle First National
   Bank
Spokane, WA 98102

Clayton Silver Mines, Inc.

CAPITALIZATION:
Capital stock, par value 10¢ per share; 3,500,000 shares authorized and 3,000,000 shares outstanding.

DESCRIPTION OF COMPANY:
The Clayton Silver mine is a group of 36 claims in Bayhorse Mining District near the town of Clayton, Custer County, Idaho. It has been a steady producer of silver-lead-zinc ore for many years. About 70% of its mining income is from silver. Company owns 173,989 shares of Sunshine Mining, 70,067 shares of Consolidated Silver, 73,974 Metropolitan Mines and 77,500 Vindicator.

OPINION:
One of the top rated junior silver producers that is underpriced at this stage of the market.

PRICE HISTORY:

YEAR	HIGH	LOW
1972	.78	.47
1973	1.30	.50
1974	2.25	.70
1975	1.50	.75
1976	1.10	.75
1977	1.30	.74
1978	1.00	.61
1979	3.50	.66
1980	4.50	1.80
1981	3.15	1.25
1982 to date	2.00	1.10

Coeur d'Alene
Crescent
Mining
Company

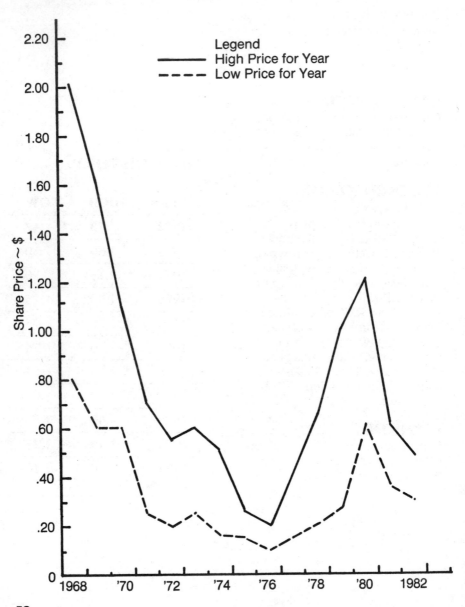

Spokane OTC
Inc. 1973
Idaho

P.O. Box 469
Wallace, ID 83873
Pres. – Walter L. Sly
Sec. – D.L. Hess

Transfer Agent:
H.F. Magnuson & Co.
P.O. Box 469
Wallace, ID 83873

Coeur d'Alene Crescent Mining Company

CAPITALIZATION:

One class of outstanding securities consisting of 5,000,000 shares of authorized nonassessable capital stock with a par value of 2½ ¢ per share. As of December 31, 1981, there were 3,058,285 shares of stock issued and outstanding.

DESCRIPTION OF COMPANY:

The company's business consists of the ownership of mining claims located in Shoshone County, Idaho. The property of the company consists of one unpatented and six patented mining claims and a patented millsite located about 1 mile west of Osburn, Idaho. Owns 756,976 shares of Metropolitan Mines, 75,000 shares of Burke Mining and 50,000 shares of Lucky Star.

OPINION:

Because of its property holdings and its stockholdings in other companies, CDA Crescent would have to be considered a buy.

PRICE HISTORY:

YEAR	HIGH	LOW
1968	2.00	.80
1969	1.60	.60
1970	1.10	.60
1971	.70	.25
1972	.55	.20
1973	.60	.25
1974	.50	.16
1975	.26	.15
1976	.20	.10
1977	.42	.15
1978	.65	.20
1979	1.00	.27
1980	1.20	.60
1981	.60	.35
1982 to date	.48	.30

Coeur d'Alene Mines Corporation

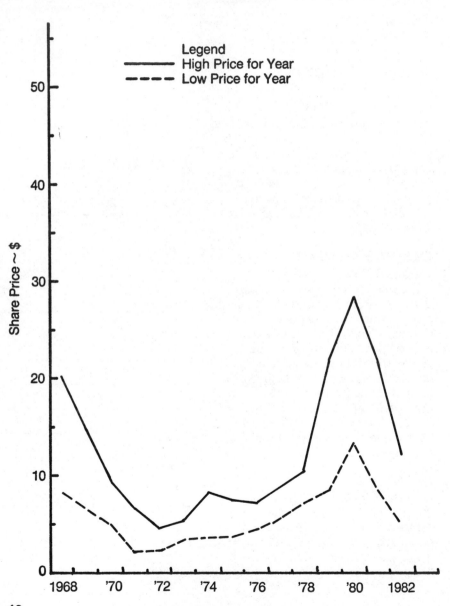

Spokane OTC
Inc. 1928
Idaho

P.O. Box 889
Wallace, ID 83873
Pres.—Dennis E. Wheeler

Transfer Agent:
416 River St.
Wallace, ID 83873
(208) 556-1121

Coeur d'Alene Mines Corporation

CAPITALIZATION:
Nonassessable common stock with par value of $1 each— 10,000,000 shares, of which 5,165,897 were issued and outstanding on December 31, 1981.

DESCRIPTION OF COMPANY:
Its Coeur mine is third largest primary silver mine in U.S. 1981 yield, 2,592,700 ounces; first half 1982 production, 1,247,000 ounces silver and 1,185,000 pounds copper. Ore reserves totaled over 1.3 million tons averaging 18.4 oz. silver and .9% copper per ton. Under ASARCO's operation, Coeur is lowest cost underground silver mine in the district. CDA Mines has 12.1% interest in nearby Consolidated Silver lease and 7.69% of Con Sil shares. Also owns 49.8% of Royal Apex Silver and varying interests in ASARCO's American Silver Project adjoining the Coeur mine.

OPINION:
Is one of the most attractive of the larger silver mining companies and should be rated a top buy.

PRICE HISTORY:

YEAR	HIGH	LOW
1968	20.00	8.00
1969	14.50	6.25
1970	9.25	4.75
1971	6.50	2.00
1972	4.50	2.25
1973	5.25	3.25
1974	8.00	3.50
1975	7.25	3.50
1976	7.00	4.25
1977	8.50	5.25
1978	10.25	7.00
1979	21.50	8.25
1980	28.00	13.00
1981	21.50	8.50
1982 to date	12.00	5.00

Conjecture Mines Inc.

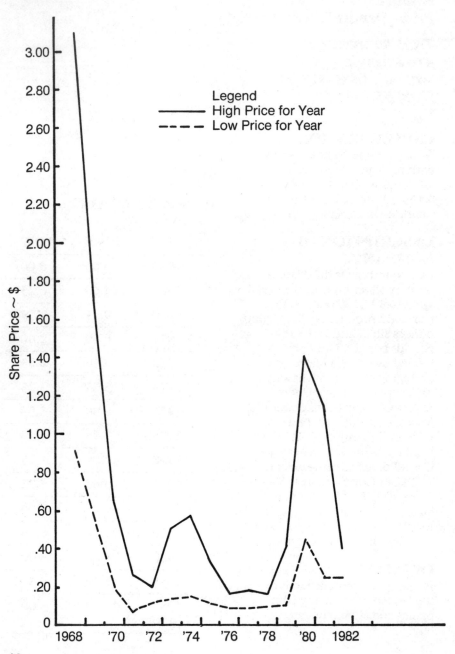

Spokane OTC
Inc. 1954
Idaho

212 Symons Bldg.
Spokane, WA 99204
Pres. – Robert B. Austin
Sec. – Lyle Funnell

Transfer Agent:
Le Master & Daniels
212 Symons Bldg.
Spokane, WA 99204

Conjecture Mines Inc.

CAPITALIZATION:
5,000,000 shares at 10¢ par value. Issued and outstanding: 4,938,085 shares.

DESCRIPTION OF COMPANY:
The Conjecture mine property of about 100 claims is 4 miles south of Lakeview, Lake Pend Oreille, Idaho, and northwest of Coeur d'Alene Mining District. Initial silver-lead shipments made before turn of the century. Considerable development work done by Federal Resources Corp. and Duval Corp. in 1960s. Minerals Management, Inc. a Delaware firm, has been preparing the mine for production since April, 1979. Conjecture would receive one-third of profits.

OPINION:
One of the more attractive of the junior silver stocks in a rising silver market.

PRICE HISTORY:

YEAR	HIGH	LOW
1968	3.10	.90
1969	1.70	.55
1970	.65	.20
1971	.26	.08
1972	.20	.12
1973	.50	.14
1974	.57	.15
1975	.33	.12
1976	.17	.09
1977	.18	.09
1978	.16	.10
1979	.42	.11
1980	1.40	.45
1981	1.15	.25
1982 to date	.40	.25

Consolidated Silver Corp.

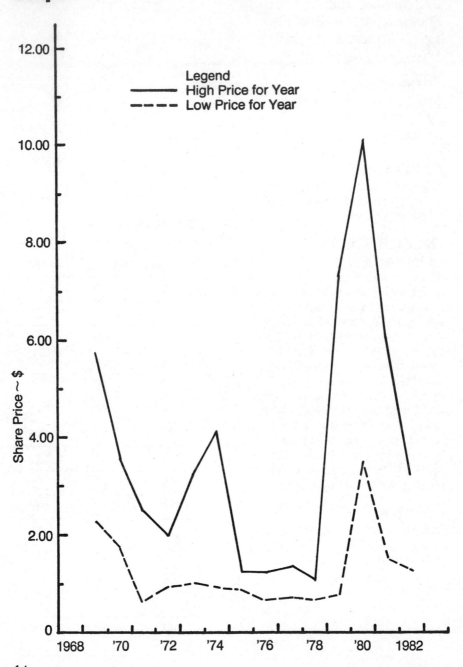

Spokane OTC
Inc. 1968
Idaho

P.O. Box 320
Wallace, ID 83873
Pres. – Alden Hull
Sec. – William J. Grismer

Transfer Agent:
P.O. Box 320
Wallace, ID 83873

Consolidated Silver Corp.

CAPITALIZATION:

Authorized 10,000,000 shares of nonassessable common stock, par value 10¢ each and 12,500 shares of redeemable preferred stock, $100 par value each; 8,205,689 common shares issued and outstanding.

DESCRIPTION OF COMPANY:

Owns large group of claims east of Sunshine mine. Includes Silver Summit mine, mill and surface plant formerly owned and operated by Hecla; also mineral properties formerly owned by Yakima Shoshone, Silver Dollar, Lincoln, Silver Chieftain, Plainview, Merger and Coeur d'Alene Mines. Hecla current lessee operator with Sunshine and CDA Mines as joint venture partners in deepening shaft and developing new ore reserves.

OPINION:

One of the most attractive of the medium sized silver mining companies because of its property position in the CDA District and because the shares are so closely held. Definitely a buy.

PRICE HISTORY:

YEAR	HIGH	LOW
1969	5.75	2.25
1970	3.50	1.75
1971	2.50	.63
1972	2.00	.90
1973	3.25	1.00
1974	4.10	.90
1975	1.25	.90
1976	1.25	.65
1977	1.35	.70
1978	1.05	.65
1979	7.25	.75
1980	10.00	3.50
1981	6.00	1.50
1982 to date	3.20	1.25

Daybreak Mines, Inc.

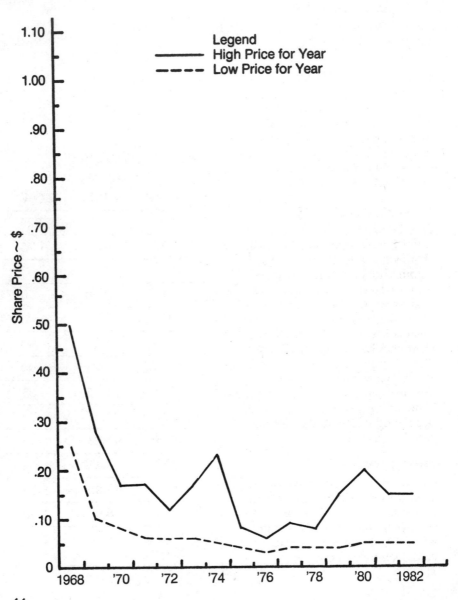

Spokane OTC
Inc. 1955
Idaho

P.O. Box 370
Osburn, ID 83849
Pres. –Earl Tenley
Sec. –Dale LaVinge

Transfer Agent:
P.O. Box 370
Osburn, ID 83849

Daybreak Mines, Inc.

CAPITALIZATION:
Authorized 6,000,000 shares of capital stock having a par value of 10¢ per share. Issued and outstanding: 5,960,357 shares.

DESCRIPTION OF COMPANY:
First mined uranium ore from leased property near Mt. Spokane in 1950s. Subsequently acquired claims totaling 760 acres on both sides of Osburn Fault between Osburn and Silverton, Idaho. Southern boundary only 4,000 feet from Coeur mine shaft. Two mineralized zones exposed. Well financed operator being sought. Owns 357,094 shares of Silver Hill Mines and 41,926 shares of Sidney Mining.

OPINION:
Company property is strategically located on the Osburn Fault so investors who will be looking for key issues in the CDA Silver Mining District will have to pay attention to this one.

PRICE HISTORY:

YEAR	HIGH	LOW
1968	.50	.25
1969	.28	.10
1970	.17	.08
1971	.17	.06
1972	.12	.06
1973	.17	.06
1974	.23	.05
1975	.08	.04
1976	.06	.03
1977	.09	.04
1978	.08	.04
1979	.15	.04
1980	.20	.05
1981	.15	.05
1982 to date	.15	.05

East Coeur d'Alene Silver Mines, Inc.

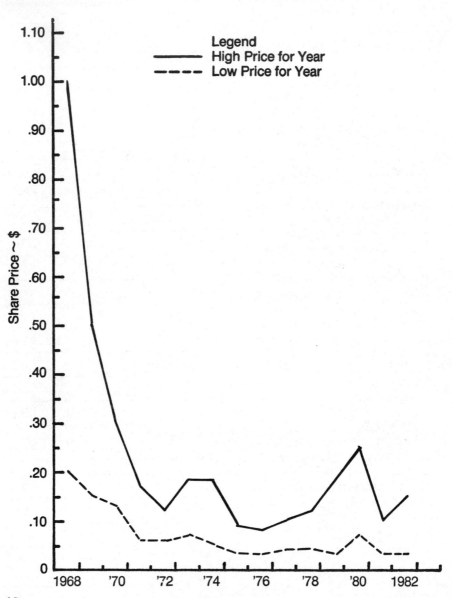

Spokane OTC
Inc. 1961
Idaho

P.O. Box 469
Wallace, ID 83873
Pres.–H.F. Magnuson
Sec.–D.L. Hess

Transfer Agent:
H.F. Magnuson & Co.
P.O. Box 469
Wallace, ID 83873

East Coeur d'Alene Silver Mines, Inc.

CAPITALIZATION:

One class of outstanding securities consisting of 10,000,000 shares of authorized nonassessable capital stock with a par value of 10¢ per share. As of December 31, 1981, there were 5,938,624 shares of stock issued and outstanding.

DESCRIPTION OF COMPANY:

Organized to explore 103 claims adjacent to Nancy Lee mine near Superior, Montana, but leased them to Nancy Lee Mines in 1966. Then staked 22 claims 3 miles south of Galena mine and 14 claims south of Bismarck property, both in CDA Mining District, which were leased to Sunshine in 1967.

OPINION:

One of the many interesting penny silver stocks that could do better with higher silver prices.

PRICE HISTORY:

YEAR	HIGH	LOW
1968	1.00	.20
1969	.50	.15
1970	.30	.13
1971	.17	.06
1972	.12	.06
1973	.18	.07
1974	.18	.05
1975	.09	.03
1976	.08	.03
1977	.10	.04
1978	.12	.04
1979	.18	.03
1980	.25	.07
1981	.10	.03
1982 to date	.15	.03

Eastern
Star
Mining
Company

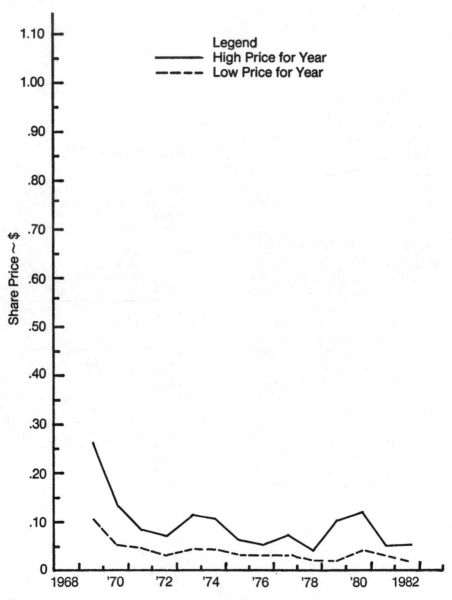

Spokane OTC
Inc. 1906
Idaho

P.O. Box 488
202 Johnston Bldg.
Coeur d'Alene, ID 83814
Pres. – Dr. Robert Reid

Transfer Agent:
Spokane Guaranty Co.
1306 Washington Mutual
  Bldg.
Spokane, WA 99201

Eastern Star Mining Company

CAPITALIZATION:
Common stock 10¢ par value:
5,000,000 shares authorized and
4,484,595 shares issued and outstanding.

DESCRIPTION OF COMPANY:
The company has obtained all of
its existing properties in
exchange for common stock.
The company controls 20 unpatented mining claims located
in Madison County, Montana,
Rochester Mining District; 19 unpatented mining claims located
in Sanders County, Montana; and
has an interest in a block of
claims on the east end of the
Coeur d'Alene Mining District,
located in Mineral County,
Montana.

OPINION:
None.

PRICE HISTORY:

YEAR	HIGH	LOW
1969	.26	.10
1970	.13	.05
1971	.08	.04
1972	.07	.03
1973	.11	.04
1974	.10	.04
1975	.06	.03
1976	.05	.03
1977	.07	.03
1978	.04	.02
1979	.10	.02
1980	.12	.04
1981	.05	.03
1982 to date	.05	.02

Empire Explorations, Inc.

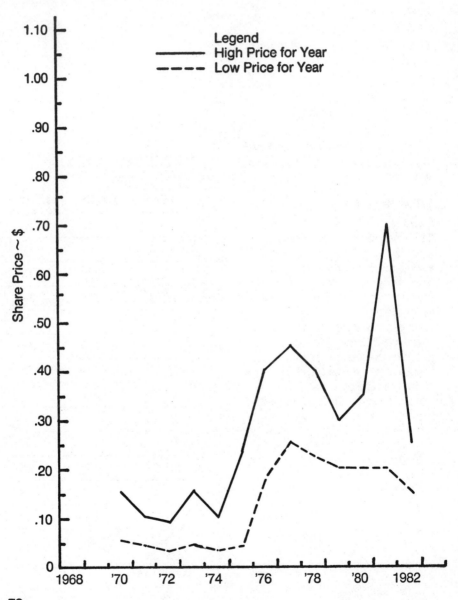

Spokane OTC
Inc. 1967
Washington

609 Hutton Bldg.
Spokane, WA 99204
Pres.–Maynard J. Davies
Sec.–James Webbert

Transfer Agent:
609 Hutton Bldg.
Spokane, WA 99204

Empire Explorations, Inc.

CAPITALIZATION:
Capital stock 3,000,000 shares
10¢ par value authorized. Issued
and outstanding: 2,731,500
shares.

DESCRIPTION OF COMPANY:
In 1968 acquired the 12-claim
Silver Empire property which
adjoins on the south the Silverore Mines property in which
Sunshine Mining has core-drilled
silver mineralization. Empire Ex.
has done bulldozing and soil
sampling. Also has claims in
Springdale Mining District,
Stevens County, Washington, oil
and gas leases in east central
Washington and some oil
revenue from Montana wells.

OPINION:
Is an attractive penny silver
stock in the Coeur d'Alene
Region. High stock prices could
be anticipated with a major
move in silver.

PRICE HISTORY:

YEAR	HIGH	LOW
1970	.15	.05
1971	.10	.04
1972	.09	.03
1973	.15	.04
1974	.10	.03
1975	.23	.04
1976	.40	.18
1977	.45	.25
1978	.40	.22
1979	.30	.20
1980	.40	.20
1981	.70	.20
1982 to date	.25	.15

Fourth of July Silver, Inc.

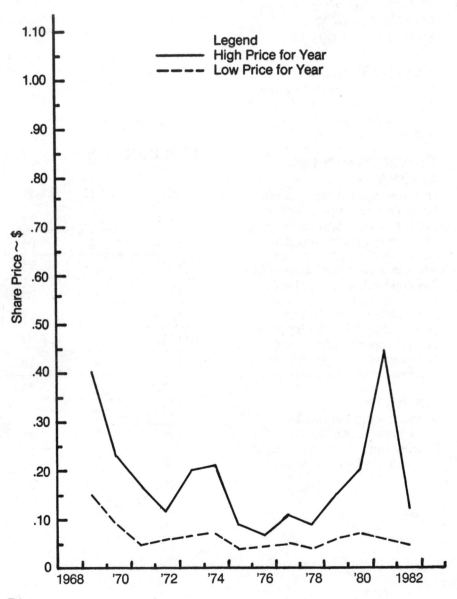

Spokane Stock Exchange
Inc. 1968
Idaho

P.O. Box 212
Hunter Ranch Add.
Mullan, ID 83846
(208) 744-1637
Pres. – W.E. Hayes
Sec. – Norm Brock

Transfer Agent:
Spokane Guaranty Co.
1306 Washington Mutual
*   Bldg.*
Spokane, WA 99201

Fourth of July Silver, Inc.

CAPITALIZATION:

Authorized 5,000,000 common stock, 10¢ par value per share, nonassessable. Issued and outstanding: 1,657,820 shares.

DESCRIPTION OF COMPANY:

Owns 21 contiguous unpatented silver, lead and copper mining claims in the St. Joe Mining District, Shoshone County, Idaho, at the confluence of Bullion Creek and Wonderful Creek and 4 miles east of Bullion Creek's confluence with the North Fork of the St. Joe River. Owns 170,000 shares of Antimony Mining & Milling.

OPINION:

One of the listed penny silver stocks that probably has more silver in the name than in the properties.

PRICE HISTORY:

YEAR	HIGH	LOW
1969	.40	.15
1970	.23	.09
1971	.17	.05
1972	.12	.06
1973	.20	.07
1974	.21	.07
1975	.09	.04
1976	.07	.04
1977	.11	.05
1978	.09	.04
1979	.15	.06
1980	.20	.07
1981	.44	.06
1982 to date	.12	.05

Golden Eagle Mining Company

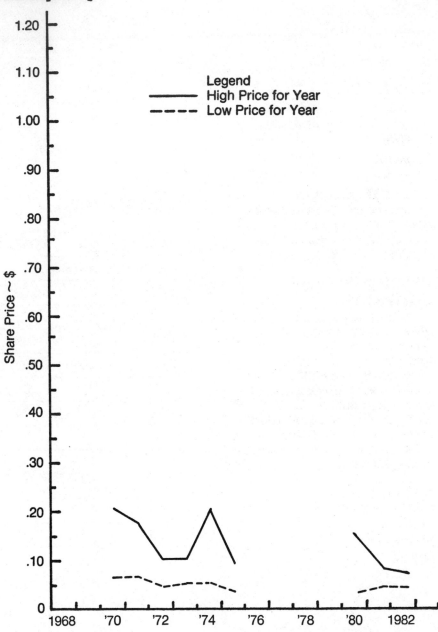

Legend
—— High Price for Year
---- Low Price for Year

Share Price ~ $

1.20
1.10
1.00
.90
.80
.70
.60
.50
.40
.30
.20
.10
0

1968 '70 '72 '74 '76 '78 '80 1982

Spokane OTC
Inc. 1968
Idaho

504½ Bank St.
P.O. Box 1127
Wallace, ID 83873
Pres. – Frank Morbeck
Sec./Treas. – Virginia
Mattern

Transfer Agent:
504½ Bank St.
P.O. Box 1127
Wallace, ID 83873

Golden Eagle Mining Company

CAPITALIZATION:
Capital stock authorized:
9,000,000 shares at 10¢ par
value, 6,314,500 shares issued
and outstanding.

DESCRIPTION OF COMPANY:
The company owns one
patented mining claim and five
unpatented claims in the Neihart
Mining District in Montana. The
company also owns three
patented claims in Rimini as well
as 10 unpatented claims in the
Murray Mining District. There
have been additional soil sampling and development on the
High Tariff claims near Neihart
in Montana. The company leased
the High Tariff claims consisting
of one patented and one unpatented to Cominco American
Mining Co. in 1981.

OPINION:
None.

PRICE HISTORY:

YEAR	HIGH	LOW
1970	.20	.06
1971	.17	.06
1972	.10	.04
1973	.10	.05
1974	.20	.05
1975	.09	.03
1976		
1977		
1978		
1979		
1980	.15	.03
1981	.08	.04
1982 to date	.07	.04

Grandview Mines Company

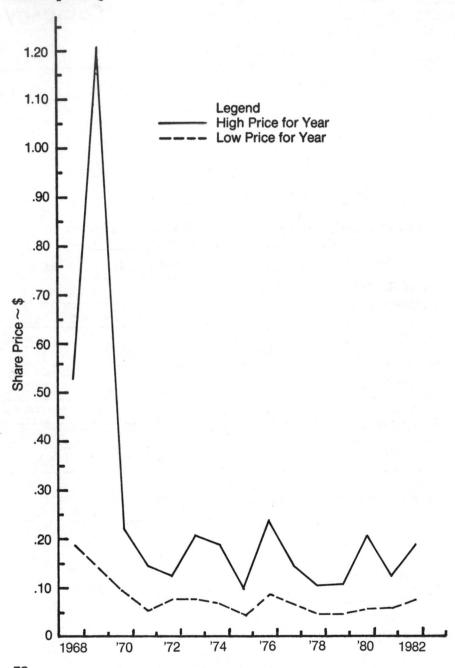

Spokane Stock Exchange Inc. 1927
Idaho

Columbia Building
Spokane, WA 99201
Pres.–Karl W. Jasper
Sec.–E.K. Barnes

Transfer Agent:
Spokane Guaranty Co.
1306 Washington Mutual
  Bank Bldg.
Spokane, WA 99201

Grandview Mines Company

CAPITALIZATION:
Recapitalized from 6,000,000 authorized shares at 10¢ par to 30,000,000 shares no par value; 4,086,630 issued and outstanding.

DESCRIPTION OF COMPANY:
Owns mining claims or mineral rights covering about 5,000 acres in Stevens County, Washington, including Scandia zinc mine. Owns over 100,000 shares of Little Squaw Gold and 80,000 Capitol Silver. Also large portfolio of South African gold stocks.

OPINION:
None.

PRICE HISTORY:

YEAR	HIGH	LOW
1968	.52	.18
1969	1.20	.36
1970	.22	.09
1971	.14	.05
1972	.12	.07
1973	.20	.07
1974	.18	.06
1975	.09	.04
1976	.23	.08
1977	.14	.06
1978	.10	.04
1979	.10	.04
1980	.20	.05
1981	.12	.05
1982 to date	.18	.07

Gulf Resources & Chemical Co.

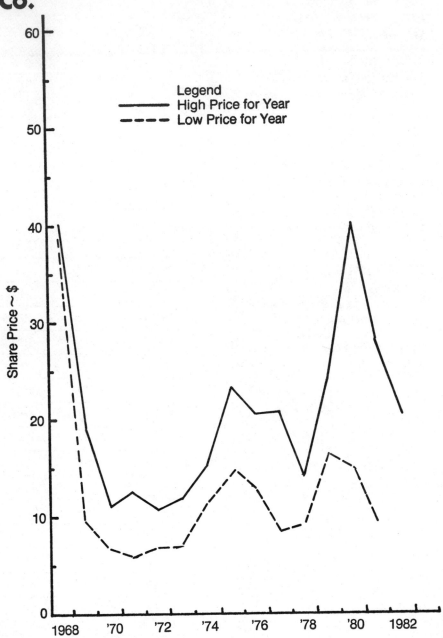

Gulf Resources & Chemical Co.

47th Floor, 1100 Milam
*   Building*
Houston, TX 77002
Pres. –A.E. Clore

Transfer Agent:
First City National Bank
*   of Houston*
Suite 615, 909 Fannin St.
P.O. Box 3856
Houston, TX 77001

CAPITALIZATION:

Preferred stock, $1 par, author-
ized 4,000,000 shares. Common
stock, 10¢ par, authorized
20,000,000 shares; outstanding,
8,969,076 shares.

DESCRIPTION OF COMPANY:

A diversified Houston, Texas,
company which in 1968 took
over The Bunker Hill Co., Kellogg, Idaho, mining, smelting
and refining firm with more than
2,000 employees. Because of
low lead-zinc-silver prices and
operating losses, Gulf phased out
Bunker Hill operations in late
1981 and 1982.

OPINION:

Could not now be considered a
silver stock because of
permanent closure of Bunker
Hill.

PRICE HISTORY:

YEAR	HIGH	LOW
1968	40.00	38.50
1969	19.25	9.50
1970	11.00	6.75
1971	12.50	5.75
1972	10.75	5.50
1973	12.00	6.75
1974	15.25	6.65
1975	23.25	11.25
1976	20.50	14.50
1977	20.75	12.50
1978	14.00	8.50
1979	24.00	9.25
1980	40.00	16.50
1981	28.00	15.00
1982 to date	20.50	9.65

Hecla
Mining
Company

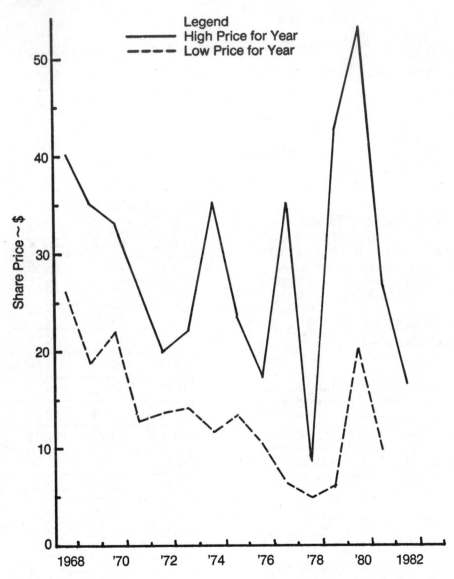

Legend
— High Price for Year
---- Low Price for Year

DAY MINES, INC.
Effective October 20, 1981 Day
Mines, Inc. was acquired by
Hecla Mining Company on the
basis of 1.8 shares of Hecla
common stock in exchange for
each outstanding share of Day
Mines, Inc.

New York Stock Exchange
Spokane Stock Exchange
Pacific Stock Exchange
Inc. 1898
Washington

Hecla Mining Company

Hecla Building
Wallace, ID 83873
Pres. – William A. Griffith

Transfer Agent:
Seattle-First National
  Bank
Stock Transfer Dept.
P.O. Box 24186
Exchange Building
Seattle, WA 98124

CAPITALIZATION:
Preferred stock, authorized
1,000,000 shares, no stated
value. Common stock, 25¢ par
value. Authorized 20,000,000
shares; issued and outstanding,
17,730,244.

DESCRIPTION OF COMPANY:
Acquisition of Day Mines
through merger in 1981 moved
Hecla into first place among U.S.
silver mining companies ahead
of ASARCO, Inc. Silver produced
by Hecla and for its account in
1981 totaled 5.7 million ounces
or 15% of total U.S. production
of newly mined silver. Its Lucky
Friday mine ranked No. 4 among
U.S. silver producing mines with
2,253,818 ounces, and output is
expected to be increased substantially with completion of the
new Silver Shaft. Hecla owns
33½% interest in main producing area of Sunshine mine,
largest U.S. silver producer; 64%

PRICE HISTORY:

YEAR	HIGH	LOW
1968	40.00	26.00
1969	35.00	18.75
1970	33.00	21.75
1971	26.25	12.75
1972	20.00	13.50
1973	22.00	14.00
1974	35.00	11.50
1975	23.50	13.25
1976	17.00	10.50
1977	35.00	6.75
1978	8.75	4.75
1979	42.50	6.00
1980	53.00	20.00
1981	26.50	9.50
1982 to date	16.50	7.50

interest in Consolidated Silver
mine; 12% of Galena mine net
profits; 5% of Coeur mine pro-
ceeds; 100% of gold mines at
Republic, Washington, 60% of a
Leadville, Colorado, silver mine;
a Nevada copper-silver mine and
other mining interests.

OPINION:
The premier silver stock in the
U.S.

Helena Silver Mines, Inc.

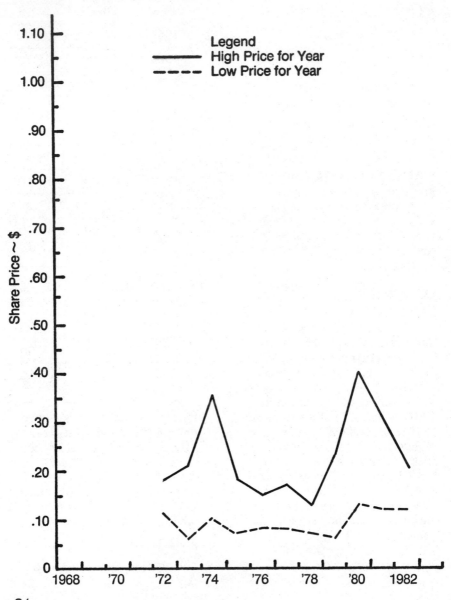

Helena Silver Mines, Inc.

Spokane Stock Exchange Inc. 1888 Montana

P.O. Box 488
Coeur d'Alene, ID 83814
Pres. –Peter W. Laczay
Sec. –H.S. Sanderson

Transfer Agent:
P.O. Box 488
Coeur d'Alene, ID 83814

CAPITALIZATION:
Common stock having a par value of 5¢ per share, authorized 5,000,000 shares, of which 3,494,685 shares are issued and outstanding.

DESCRIPTION OF COMPANY:
Its Gregory mine, early-day gold-silver-lead producer near Helena, Montana, is undergoing pilot testing of dump material by lessee operator. Company's leased Mammoth property in Montana's Judith Mountain Gold District is under a 1980 operating agreement to Gold Cache, Inc. A 30-claim prospect in St. Joe Mining District south of CDA District recently leased to Bear Creek Mining Co. Also owns half interest in Mary Ingabar gold mine near Whitehall, Montana.

OPINION:
None.

PRICE HISTORY:

YEAR	HIGH	LOW
1972	.18	.11
1973	.21	.06
1974	.35	.10
1975	.18	.07
1976	.15	.08
1977	.17	.08
1978	.13	.07
1979	.23	.06
1980	.40	.13
1981	.30	.12
1982 to date	.20	.12

85

Hibernia
Silver
Mines,
Inc.

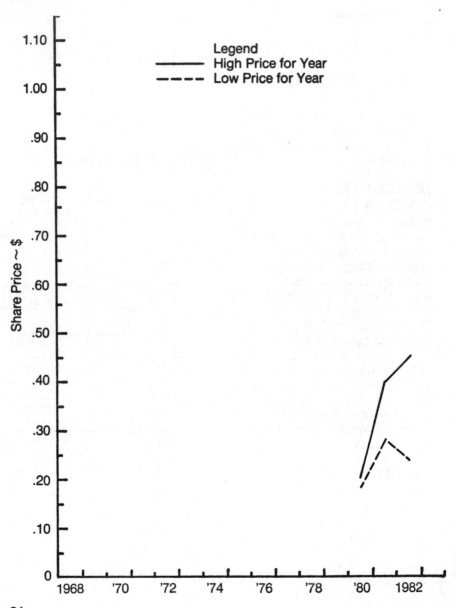

Spokane OTC
Inc. 1965
Nevada

615 Central Avenue West
Suite 1
Great Falls, MT 59404
Pres. – Dorothy Hatfield

Transfer Agent:
615 Central Avenue West
Suite 1
Great Falls, MT 59404

Hibernia Silver Mines, Inc.

CAPITALIZATION:
Authorized 5,000,000 shares of which all are issued and out-standing.

DESCRIPTION OF COMPANY:
Hibernia property consists of five unpatented claims lying north of the Lucky Friday and Vindicator properties and adjoining Abot, Silver Mountain and Day Mines (Hecla).

OPINION:
Because of its strategic location by the Lucky Friday mine, Hibernia has been attracting buying in recent times. The stock appears to be closely held and could sell higher in more active silver markets.

PRICE HISTORY:

YEAR	HIGH	LOW
1980	.20	.18
1981	.40	.28
1982 to date	.45	.24

Highland Surprise Consolidated Mining Company

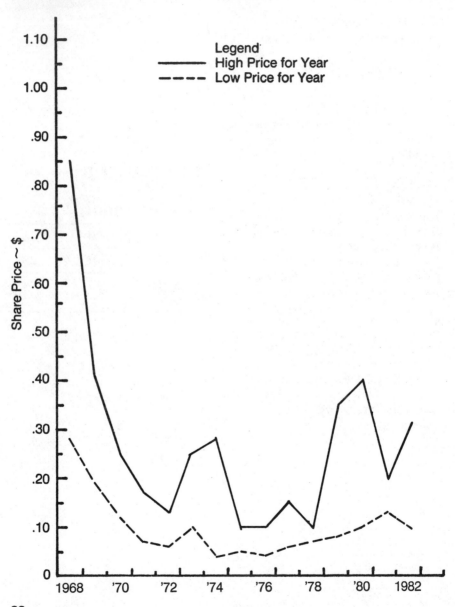

Spokane OTC
Inc. 1912
Idaho

P.O. Box 469
Wallace, ID 83873
Pres.–J.B. Colson
Sec.–D.L. Hess

Transfer Agent:
H.F. Magnuson & Co.
P.O. Box 469
Wallace, ID 83873

Highland Surprise Consolidated Mining Company

CAPITALIZATION:

5,000,000 shares of authorized capital stock with a par value of 15¢ per share. As of October 31, 1981, there were 2,479,704 shares of stock issued and outstanding.

DESCRIPTION OF COMPANY:

Owns 12 patented and 60 un-patented mining claims in the Yreka Mining District, Shoshone County, Idaho, and also holds the J.D. Group of 20 unpatented mining claims located near Superior, Montana. In addition to the above mining claims, the company holds an interest in the Bryden-Prue Oil lease near Cushing, Oklahoma.

OPINION:

With interest coming into the penny mining stocks, Highland Surprise could sell higher easier than some of the others because of its small capitalization.

PRICE HISTORY:

YEAR	HIGH	LOW
1968	.85	.28
1969	.41	.19
1970	.25	.12
1971	.17	.07
1972	.13	.06
1973	.25	.10
1974	.28	.04
1975	.10	.05
1976	.10	.04
1977	.15	.06
1978	.10	.07
1979	.35	.08
1980	.40	.10
1981	.20	.13
1982 to date	.31	.10

Hunter Creek Mining Company

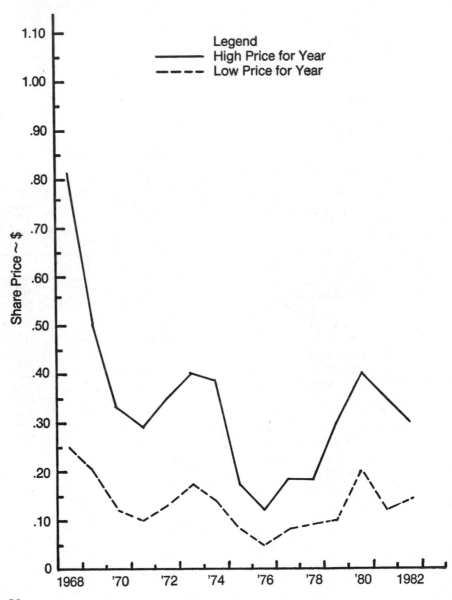

Spokane OTC
Inc. 1945
Idaho

P.O. Box 487
Portland, OR 97210
(503) 227-3277
Pres. –M.W. Onstine
Sec./Treas. –Karl W. Jasper

Transfer Agent:
P.O. Box 487
Portland, OR 97207

Hunter Creek Mining Company

CAPITALIZATION:
3,500,000 authorized shares, 10¢ par value, nonassessable stock; 3,488,000 shares issued and outstanding. There are approximately 2,000 shareholders.

DESCRIPTION OF COMPANY:
Its nine unpatented claims border Hecla's Lucky Friday mine property on the north. Hecla, which has a half interest under an old agreement, extended Lucky Friday's 1400-foot level into Hunter Creek in 1947 but has done little exploration since. Also has a half interest in Dayton-Inspiration Gold, Silver City, Nevada.

OPINION:
Has always proved to be one of the more attractive silver mining stocks when the market is running because of the strategic location of its property.

PRICE HISTORY:

YEAR	HIGH	LOW
1968	.81	.25
1969	.50	.20
1970	.33	.12
1971	.29	.10
1972	.35	.13
1973	.40	.17
1974	.38	.14
1975	.17	.08
1976	.12	.05
1977	.18	.08
1978	.18	.09
1979	.30	.10
1980	.40	.20
1981	.35	.12
1982 to date	.30	.14

Idaho General Mines, Inc.

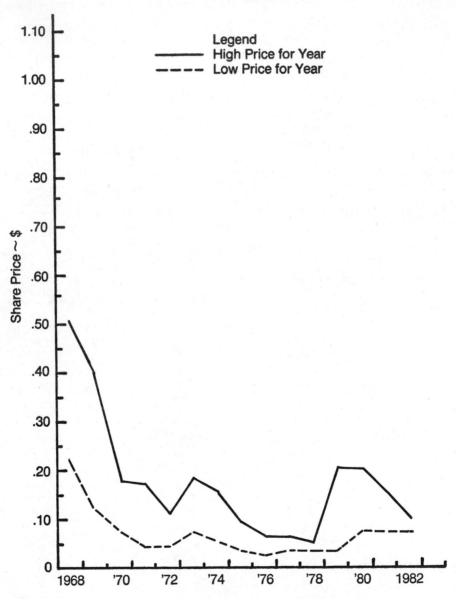

Spokane OTC
Inc. 1925
Idaho

P.O. Box 709
Wallace, ID 83873
Pres.–Piatt Hull
Sec.–Mary Nash

Transfer Agent:
P.O. Box 709
Wallace, ID 83873

Idaho General Mines, Inc.

CAPITALIZATION:

Capital stock, 3,000,000 shares authorized, par value 10¢ per share of which 2,986,322 shares are outstanding.

DESCRIPTION OF COMPANY:

Its CDA District property, consisting of 107 patented acres and 27 unpatented claims on Little Pine Creek adjoining ASARCO's former producing Page mine, was leased to Cominco American, Inc., in January, 1981. Three mining leases in Mayo Dist., Yukon Territory, leased in 1979 to Canada Tungsten Mining Corp., Ltd. Chicago-London group of six patented claims near Murray, Idaho, on inactive status.

OPINION:

Stock appears cheap at this time.

PRICE HISTORY:

YEAR	HIGH	LOW
1968	.50	.22
1969	.40	.12
1970	.18	.07
1971	.17	.04
1972	.11	.04
1973	.18	.07
1974	.15	.05
1975	.09	.03
1976	.06	.02
1977	.06	.03
1978	.05	.03
1979	.20	.03
1980	.20	.07
1981	.15	.07
1982 to date	.10	.07

Idaho Leadville Mines Co.

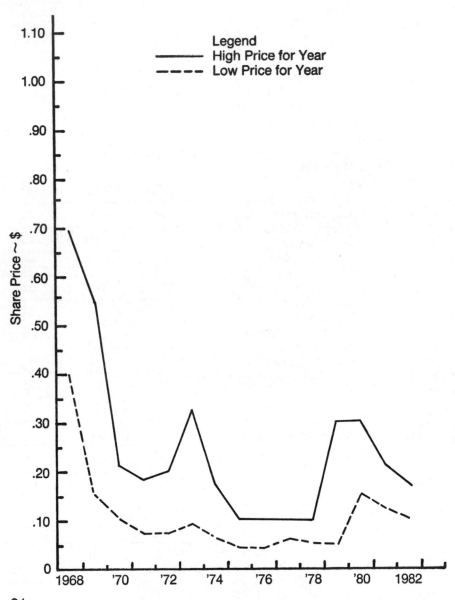

Spokane OTC
Inc. 1937
Idaho

North 910 Washington
Spokane, WA 99201
Pres. – Wm. D. Roberts
Sec. – Robert L. Patterson

Transfer Agent:
North 910 Washington
Spokane, WA 99201

Idaho Leadville Mines Co.

CAPITALIZATION:
3,000,000 shares common stock at 5¢ per share authorized and 2,067,684 issued and outstanding.

DESCRIPTION OF COMPANY:
Its 40-claim prospect south of Osburn, CDA District, unitized with adjoining Fahey group of 18 claims several years ago and operating agreement signed with Bunker Hill in 1967. That firm spent required $150,000, all on surface and in drilling nine down-holes, then surrendered agreement.

OPINION:
Has been a front runner in past bull markets on silver. Higher silver prices could take it up.

PRICE HISTORY:

YEAR	HIGH	LOW
1968	.70	.40
1969	.55	.15
1970	.21	.10
1971	.18	.07
1972	.20	.07
1973	.32	.09
1974	.17	.06
1975	.10	.04
1976	.10	.04
1977	.10	.06
1978	.10	.05
1979	.30	.05
1980	.30	.15
1981	.21	.12
1982 to date	.17	.10

Idaho Montana Silver Mines, Inc.

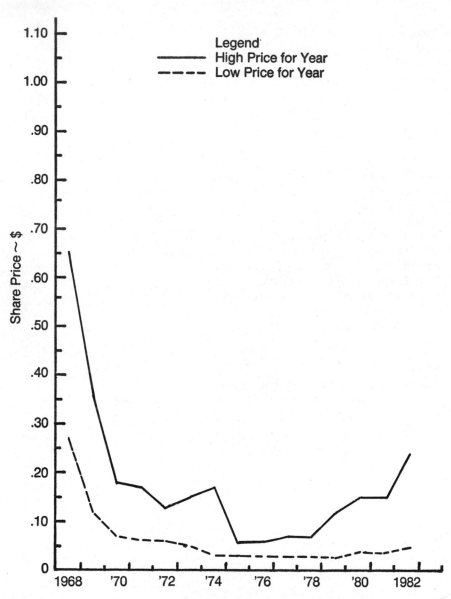

Spokane OTC
Inc. 1954
Idaho

P.O. Box 469
Wallace, ID 83873
Pres.–Wray Featherstone
Sec.–D.L. Hess

Transfer Agent:
H.F. Magunson & Co.
P.O. Box 469
Wallace, ID 83873

Idaho Montana Silver Mines, Inc.

CAPITALIZATION:
8,000,000 shares of authorized nonassessable, capital stock with a par value of 5¢ per share. As of December 31, 1981, there were 5,513,667 shares of stock issued and outstanding.

DESCRIPTION OF COMPANY:
Holds more than 100 claims along the Idaho-Montana border east of Mullan. Neighbors include Princeton and Silver Mountain properties. Only maintenance work done since Bunker Hill surrendered a lease agreement in 1972. Also holds 12 unpatented claims in Keystone District near Superior, Montana.

OPINION:
One of the more attractive penny silver stocks in a rising silver market.

PRICE HISTORY:

YEAR	HIGH	LOW
1968	.65	.27
1969	.36	.12
1970	.18	.07
1971	.17	.06
1972	.13	.06
1973	.15	.05
1974	.17	.03
1975	.06	.03
1976	.06	.03
1977	.07	.03
1978	.07	.03
1979	.12	.03
1980	.15	.04
1981	.15	.04
1982 to date	.24	.05

Idaho Silver, Inc.

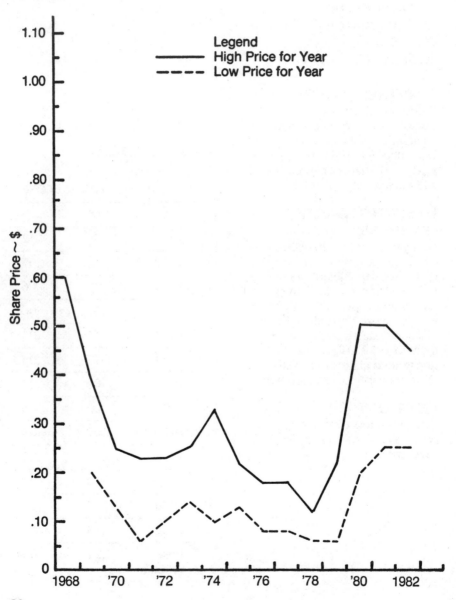

Idaho Silver, Inc.

Spokane OTC
Albert Stock Exchange
Inc. 1964
Idaho

P.O. Box 1088
Wallace, ID 83873
Pres. –Jack Scott

Transfer Agent:
P.O. Box 1088
Wallace, ID 83873

CAPITALIZATION:

Common stock, nonassessable, par value 10¢ per share, authorized 10,000,000 shares; issued and outstanding 3,430,410 shares and 3,115,410 shares, respectively, for 1981 and 1980.

DESCRIPTION OF COMPANY:

Idaho Silver owns 70 unpatented lode mining claims and a state mining lease strategically located in the Coeur d'Alene Mining District, Shoshone County, Idaho. The claims and leases are bordered to the north by Hecla Mining Company's Lucky Friday Mine and to the west and south by the Atlas Mining Company. Idaho Silver has recently acquired the K.J. silver/tin prospect in the Fort Steele Mining Division of southeastern B.C., located on the Rose Pass, 58 kilometers northeast of Nelson, B.C.

OPINION:

Obviously one of the more attractive penny silver stocks in the CDA Mining District.

PRICE HISTORY:

YEAR	HIGH	LOW
1968	.60	.20
1969	.40	.20
1970	.25	.13
1971	.23	.06
1972	.23	.10
1973	.25	.14
1974	.33	.10
1975	.22	.13
1976	.18	.08
1977	.18	.08
1978	.12	.06
1979	.22	.06
1980	.50	.20
1981	.50	.25
1982 to date	.45	.25

Independence Lead Mines Company

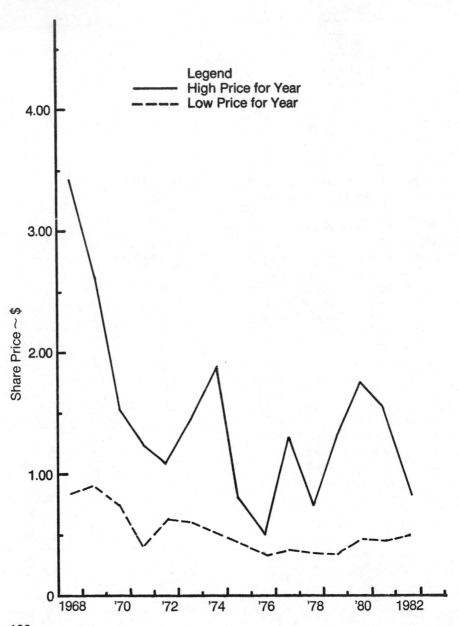

Spokane Stock Exchange Inc. 1929
Arizona

1527 Northwest Blvd.
Spokane, WA 99205
Pres.–Dr. D.M. Bush
Sec.–Charles H. Stolz

Transfer Agent:
Spokane Guaranty Co.
1306 Washington Mutual
*   Bank Bldg.*
Spokane, W 99201

Independence Lead Mines Company

CAPITALIZATION:

Common, nonassessable stock $1 par value; 4,000,000 shares authorized and 3,930,047 shares issued and outstanding.

DESCRIPTION OF COMPANY:

Its 31 claims north of Mullan, Idaho, are under exploration contract with Hecla Mining. Eastern portion unitized with Day Mines' Gold Hunter mine property, early-day producer, and Abot Mining Co. claims to the north. Hecla has been exploring the unitized area by means of a long extension of its Lucky Friday mine's 4,050-foot level.

OPINION:

This stock could work much higher with better silver prices because of the strategic location of its properties and its previous price performance.

PRICE HISTORY:

YEAR	HIGH	LOW
1968	3.40	.84
1969	2.61	.90
1970	1.55	.75
1971	1.25	.40
1972	1.10	.63
1973	1.45	.60
1974	1.85	.52
1975	.80	.42
1976	.52	.34
1977	1.30	.38
1978	.75	.35
1979	1.30	.37
1980	1.75	.45
1981	1.55	.45
1982 to date	.85	.48

Inspiration
Lead
Company,
Inc.

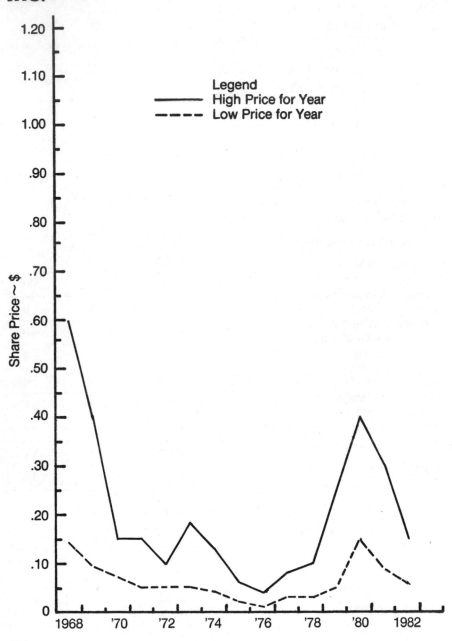

Spokane OTC
Inc. 1929, Idaho

P.O. Box 487
Portland, OR 97210
(503) 227-3277
Pres.–M.W. Onstine
Sec.–W.T. Anderson

Transfer Agent:
Burton W. Onstine
P.O. Box 487
Portland, OR 97210

Inspiration Lead Company, Inc.

CAPITALIZATION:

10,000,000 shares authorized, par value 10¢, divided into two classes of stock. Class "A" stock —5,000,000 shares authorized; issued and outstanding, 3,658,817 shares. Class "B" debenture warrant stock— 5,000,000 shares authorized; 3,000,000 issued and outstanding.

DESCRIPTION OF COMPANY:

Company owns one patented and 35 unpatented mining claims in the Evolution and Beaver Mining Districts in Shoshone County, Idaho. Silverore Mines, Inc. owns 10 unpatented and 10 patented mining claims in the same mining district. Silverore and Inspiration agreed to divide 50–50 all ore discovered on these 56 claims. The joint properties are located 2 miles northeast of Osburn, Idaho. Sunshine Mining Co., in April, 1979, entered into a revised exploration agreement covering Silverore's 20 claims and Inspiration Lead Company's 36 claims. Sunshine agreed to perform all as-

PRICE HISTORY:

YEAR	HIGH	LOW
1968	.60	.14
1969	.40	.09
1970	.15	.07
1971	.15	.05
1972	.10	.05
1973	.18	.05
1974	.13	.04
1975	.06	.02
1976	.04	.01
1977	.08	.03
1978	.10	.03
1979	.25	.05
1980	.40	.15
1981	.30	.08
1982 to date	.15	.06

sessment work, geological studies and pay the real estate taxes.

OPINION:

Because of Sunshine's interest in this company's property and its relationship geologically to the Royal-Apex and Capitol property, Inspiration is looked upon as one of the more attractive penny silver stocks.

103

Keystone
Silver
Mines,
Inc.

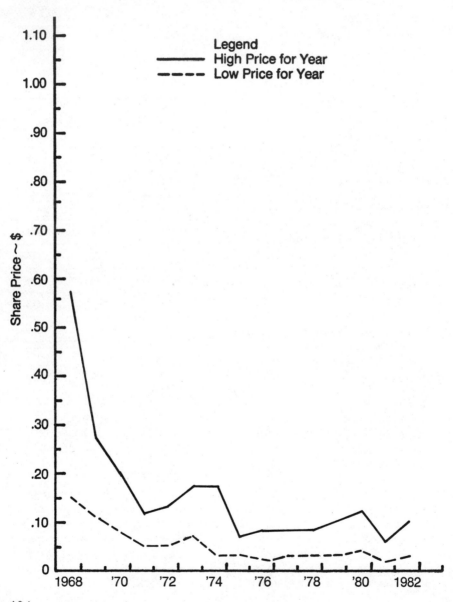

Spokane OTC
Inc. 1954
Idaho

P.O. Box 469
Wallace, ID 83873
Pres. – Piatt Hull
Sec. – D.L. Hess

Transfer Agent:
P.O. Box 469
Wallace, ID 83873

Keystone Silver Mines, Inc.

CAPITALIZATION:
10,000,000 shares of authorized nonassessable capital stock with a par value of 5¢ per share. As of December 31, 1981, there were 6,257,610 shares of stock issued and outstanding.

DESCRIPTION OF COMPANY:
Owns 56 unpatented claims and a half interest in 24 other unpatented claims near Superior, Montana, leased to Nancy Lee Mines. Also maintaining nine unpatented claims southwest of Wallace.

OPINION:
On the basis of substantial higher silver prices, interest could come back into Keystone stock.

PRICE HISTORY:

YEAR	HIGH	LOW
1968	.57	.15
1969	.27	.11
1970	.20	.08
1971	.12	.05
1972	.13	.05
1973	.17	.07
1974	.17	.03
1975	.07	.03
1976	.08	.02
1977	.08	.03
1978	.08	.03
1979	.10	.03
1980	.12	.04
1981	.06	.02
1982 to date	.10	.03

105

King of
Pine Creek
Mining
Company

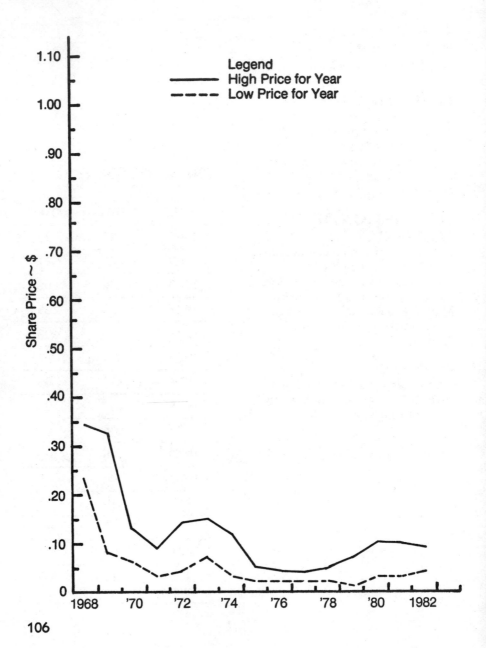

Spokane OTC
Inc. 1904
Idaho

P.O. Box 487
Portland, OR 97207
(503) 227-3277
Pres.–M.W. Onstine

Transfer Agent:
Burton W. Onstine
P.O. Box 487
Portland, OR 97207

King of Pine Creek Mining Company

CAPITALIZATION:
5,000,000 shares, par value 10¢. Issued and outstanding, 3,441,325 shares. There are approximately 500 stockholders of record.

DESCRIPTION OF COMPANY:
Owns more than 400 acres in the Pine Creek sector of the CDA District. In 1981 the company leased the land for 10 years to Cominco American, Inc. The agreement provides for a minimum annual lease payment of $1,800 or 5% royalty payments on net smelter returns, whichever is greater.

OPINION:
If Cominco goes all out to develop this company's property, further interest in the stock would be warranted.

PRICE HISTORY:

YEAR	HIGH	LOW
1968	.34	.23
1969	.32	.08
1970	.13	.06
1971	.09	.03
1972	.14	.04
1973	.15	.07
1974	.12	.03
1975	.05	.02
1976	.04	.02
1977	.04	.02
1978	.05	.02
1979	.07	.01
1980	.10	.03
1981	.10	.03
1982 to date	.09	.04

Lookout Mountain Mining & Milling Co.

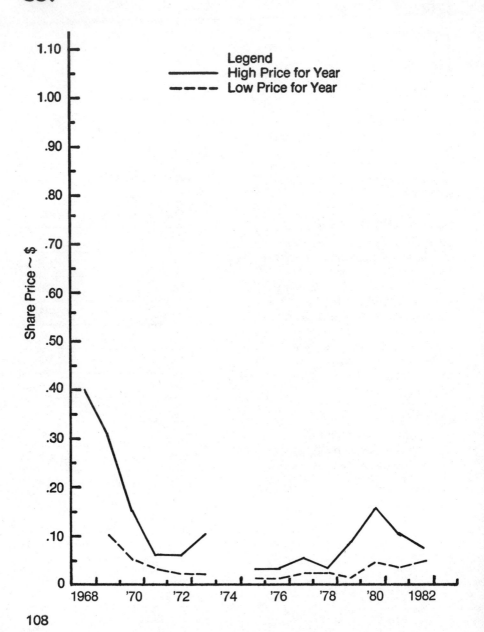

Spokane OTC
Inc. 1916
Idaho

P.O. Box 668
Coeur d'Alene, ID 83814
Pres.—Frank Morbeck
Sec.—Owen LeNore

Transfer Agent:
c/o Consolidated Metals
P.O. Box 668
Coeur d'Alene, ID 83814

CAPITALIZATION:

Authorized 6,000,000 shares of common stock with a par value of 25¢ per share, of which 5,738,951 shares are issued and outstanding.

DESCRIPTION OF COMPANY:

Has 40 claims in Pine Creek area, CDA District, adjacent to New Era Mines and Signal Silver-Gold. Also has half interest in Bi-Metallic claims near Superior, Montana, under contract to Nancy Lee Mines.

OPINION:

One of the many penny silver stocks whose price could go higher just on the basis of a major silver move.

Lookout Mountain Mining & Milling Co.

PRICE HISTORY:

YEAR	HIGH	LOW
1968	.40	.10
1969	.31	.10
1970	.15	.05
1971	.06	.03
1972	.06	.02
1973	.10	.02
1974		
1975	.03	.01
1976	.03	.01
1977	.05	.02
1978	.03	.02
1979	.08	.01
1980	.15	.04
1981	.10	.03
1982 to date	.07	.04

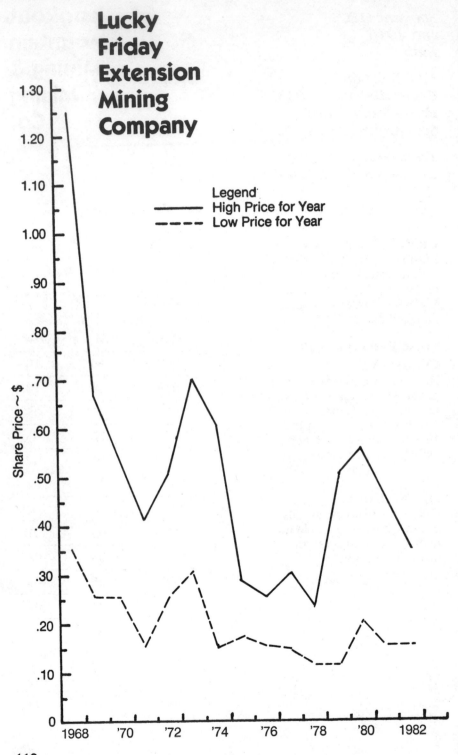

Lucky Friday Extension Mining Company

Legend
—— High Price for Year
---- Low Price for Year

Share Price ~ $

1.30
1.20
1.10
1.00
.90
.80
.70
.60
.50
.40
.30
.20
.10
0

1968 '70 '72 '74 '76 '78 '80 1982

Spokane OTC
Inc. 1945
Idaho

P.O. Box 469
Wallace, ID 83873
Pres.–D.L. Hess
Sec.–Piatt Hull

Transfer Agent:
H.F. Magnuson & Co.
P.O. Box 469
Wallace, ID 83873

Lucky Friday Extension Mining Company

CAPITALIZATION:

5,000,000 shares of authorized nonassessable capital stock with a par value of 10¢ per share; 4,049,199 shares of stock issued and outstanding.

DESCRIPTION OF COMPANY:

Owns unpatented ground adjacent to Hecla's Lucky Friday Mine. The Idaho claims of the company have been unitized with property owned by Day Mines, Inc. (Hecla) and is subject to an operating agreement with Hecla Mining. Lucky Friday Extension also holds a one-half interest in 24 additional unpatented claims located in the Keystone Mining District of Montana.

OPINION:

The name Lucky Friday has always brought buyers into it and substantially higher prices in up silver markets.

PRICE HISTORY:

YEAR	HIGH	LOW
1968	1.25	.35
1969	.67	.25
1970	.53	.25
1971	.41	.15
1972	.50	.25
1973	.70	.30
1974	.60	.15
1975	.28	.17
1976	.25	.15
1977	.30	.14
1978	.23	.11
1979	.50	.11
1980	.55	.20
1981	.45	.15
1982 to date	.35	.15

Lucky
Three
Mining
Company

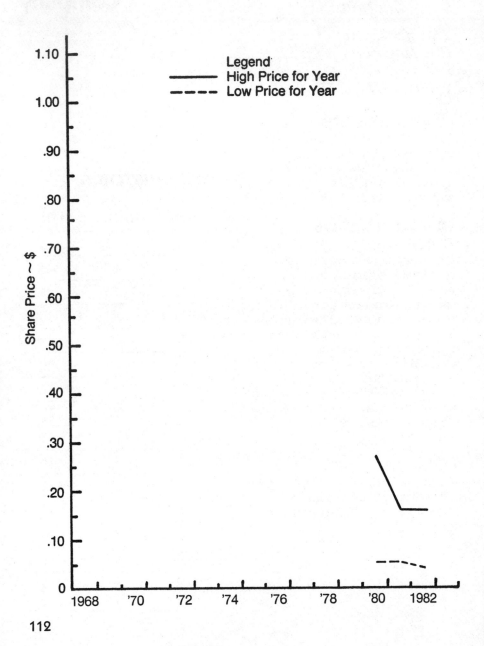

Spokane OTC
Inc. 1979
Idaho

1306 Washington Mutual
*   Bldg.*
Spokane, WA 99201
(509) 456-8710
Pres.—James B. Colson
Sec./Treas—Earl O.
*   Mithaug*

Transfer Agent:
Spokane Guaranty Co.
1306 Washington Mutual
*   Bldg.*
Spokane, WA 99201

Lucky Three Mining Company

CAPITALIZATION:
Capitalized for 15,000,000 no
par value common nonassessable
shares. During 1979 the company undertook a public offering
of its common stock and sold
4,241,400 shares at 5¢ per share.
At the present time there are
7,474,736 shares of the company's stock issued and outstanding.

DESCRIPTION OF COMPANY:
The company is in the process of
acquiring Idaho Interstate Exploration Co. which holds a
lease to 27 unpatented mining
claims in the Mud Springs Mining
District of Elko, Nevada.

OPINION:
None.

PRICE HISTORY:

YEAR	HIGH	LOW
1980	.27	.05
1981	.16	.05
1982 to date	.16	.04

Mascot Silver Lead Mines, Inc.

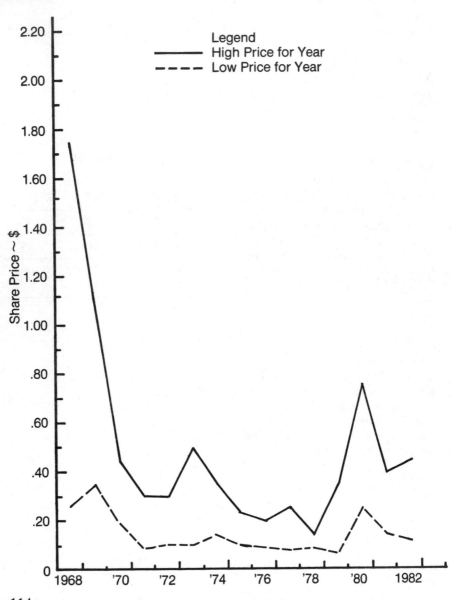

*Spokane OTC
Inc. 1950
Idaho*

*P.O. Box 660
Kellogg, ID 83837
Pres. –Ben Smick
Sec. –Ronald E. Eggart*

*Transfer Agent:
P.O. Box 660
Kellogg, ID 83873*

Mascot Silver Lead Mines, Inc.

CAPITALIZATION:
Capital stock, nonassessable with a par value of 10¢ per share; authorized 8,000,000 shares of which 5,103,495 shares are issued and outstanding.

DESCRIPTION OF COMPANY:
Its Little Pittsburg mine in Pine Creek sector of CDA District, with past production of $5 million worth of zinc lead silver, was leased early in 1982 to Cominco American. Mascot has developed silver-lead ore at Argentine-Edelweiss property and silver-lead ore at Meadow mine, both near Helena, Montana, and is closing an operating agreement with a large mining company on the former.

OPINION:
One of the more attractive of the CDA silver mining penny stocks.

PRICE HISTORY:

YEAR	HIGH	LOW
1968	1.75	.26
1969	1.10	.35
1970	.45	.19
1971	.30	.09
1972	.30	.10
1973	.50	.10
1974	.35	.14
1975	.23	.10
1976	.20	.09
1977	.25	.08
1978	.14	.09
1979	.35	.07
1980	.75	.25
1981	.40	.15
1982 to date	.45	.12

Merger
Mines
Corporation

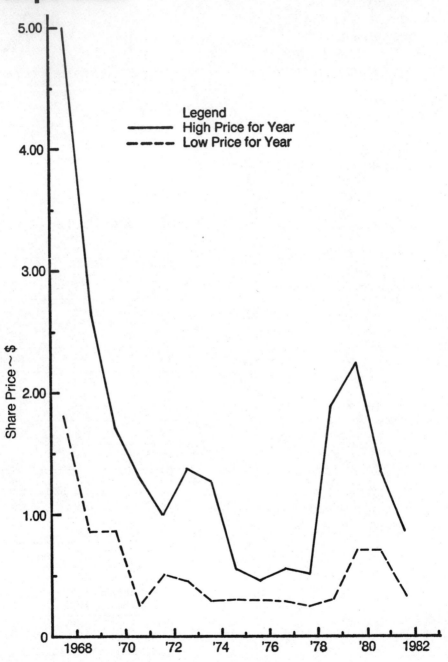

Legend
— High Price for Year
---- Low Price for Year

Share Price ~ $

Spokane OTC
Inc. 1929
Idaho

P.O. Box 716
Coeur d'Alene, ID 83814
Pres. –E.C. Gerry
Sec./Treas. –Alfred E.
 Nugent

Transfer Agent:
P.O. Box 716
Coeur d'Alene, ID 83814

Merger Mines Corporation

CAPITALIZATION:
Common stock: 10¢ par value, 3,900,000 shares authorized, of which 2,900,000 shares are issued and outstanding.

DESCRIPTION OF COMPANY:
Owns 33 patented and 12 unpatented claims in Silver Belt, CDA District, some unitized with Plainview and Coeur d'Alene Mines ground into CAMP Project and some leased to Consolidated Silver. Bear Top mine north of Murray has yielded lead-zinc-silver ore to lessee. Also owns Blacktail lode claim, same area. Has a silver prospect in northern Blaine County, Idaho. Has been exploring 19-claim Cedar Mt. lease in Kootenai County, Idaho, and Cyanide Gulch gold property, Lemhi County, Idaho. Company owns 446,810 shares of Consolidated Silver, 1,645,497 shares of Gibbonsville Premier Gold Mines, 15,000 Sidney, 83,000 Silver Crescent and 5,000 Superior Silver.

PRICE HISTORY:

YEAR	HIGH	LOW
1968	5.00	1.80
1969	2.65	.85
1970	1.70	.85
1971	1.30	.25
1972	1.00	.50
1973	1.35	.45
1974	1.25	.30
1975	.55	.30
1976	.45	.30
1977	.55	.28
1978	.50	.25
1979	1.90	.30
1980	2.25	.70
1981	1.35	.70
1982 to date	.85	.35

OPINION:
Merger should be included in any portfolio of size of low-priced silver stocks. In past markets it has demonstrated good price activity and with higher silver prices new highs could probably be reached.

117

Metaline Mining & Leasing Company

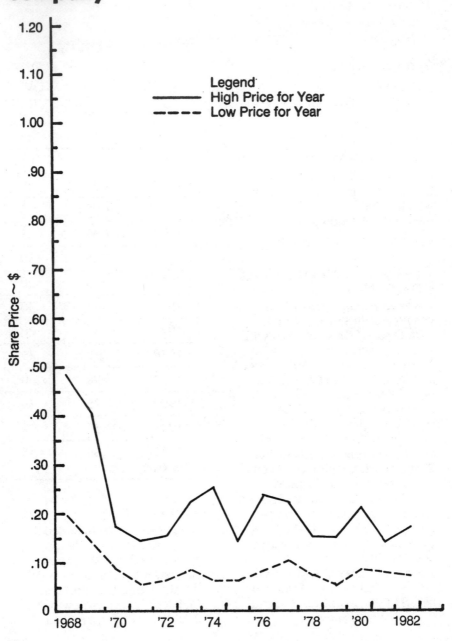

Spokane Stock Exchange
Inc. 1927
Washington

1306 Washington Mutual
*   Bank Bldg.*
Spokane, WA 99201
Pres. –Karl W. Jasper
Sec. –Maynard Irving

Transfer Agent:
Spokane Guaranty Co.
1306 Washington Mutual
*   Bank Bldg.*
Spokane, WA 99201

Metaline Mining & Leasing Company

CAPITALIZATION:
Common capital stock, 10¢ par value; 3,000,000 shares authorized and 2,987,467 shares issued and outstanding.

DESCRIPTION OF COMPANY:
Its zinc-lead properties in northeastern Washington's Metaline Mining District were sold in 1965 to Metaline Contact Mines, Inc., for 1,477,239 shares of Contact stock. Bunker Hill controlled Metaline Contact. Company also owns about 60,000 shares of Little Squaw Gold and 30,000 shares of Capitol Silver.

OPINION:
One of the more attractive listed penny silver mining stocks.

PRICE HISTORY:

YEAR	HIGH	LOW
1968	.48	.19
1969	.40	.14
1970	.17	.08
1971	.14	.05
1972	.15	.06
1973	.22	.08
1974	.25	.06
1975	.14	.06
1976	.23	.08
1977	.22	.10
1978	.15	.07
1979	.15	.05
1980	.21	.08
1981	.14	.08
1982 to date	.17	.07

Metropolitan Mines Corporation, Ltd.

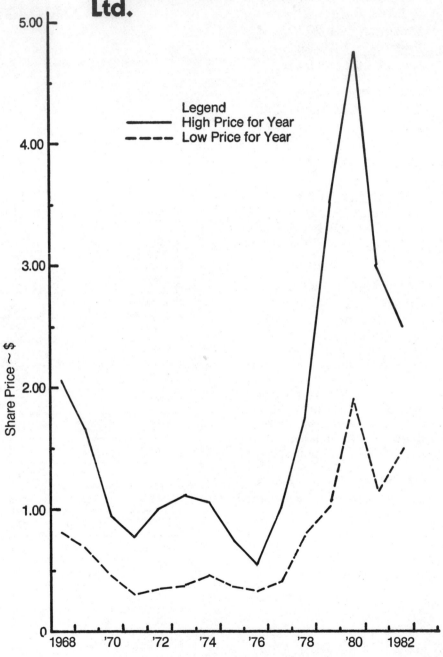

Spokane Stock Exchange
Inc. 1929
Idaho

P.O. Box 469
Wallace, ID 83873
Pres. – Wray Featherstone
Sec. – R.M. MacPhee

Transfer Agent:
Seattle-First National
*   Bank, Main Branch*
Spokane, WA 99201

Metropolitan Mines Corporation, Ltd.

CAPITALIZATION:

Capital stock Class A common stock: 4,908,415 shares are authorized, of which 3,699,919 shares are issued and outstanding, par value 10¢ per share. Capital stock, Class B common stock: 91,585 shares authorized, of which 34,485 shares are issued and outstanding, par value per share.

DESCRIPTION OF COMPANY:

Met group of 63 claims borders on the south properties of Sunshine and Consolidated Silver. Under a 1945 operating agreement, Sunshine extended 3,100 and 3,400 levels of its Sunshine mine into Met ground and mines ore from Sunshine's Yankee Girl vein, Met getting 16% of profits. In 1960s company sought to void the agreement but failed. Currently litigating over ownership of a new vein discovered at 4,000-foot depth which dips into Met ground.

PRICE HISTORY:

YEAR	HIGH	LOW
1968	2.05	.81
1969	1.65	.69
1970	.95	.46
1971	.78	.30
1972	1.00	.35
1973	1.10	.38
1974	1.05	.45
1975	.75	.37
1976	.55	.33
1977	1.00	.40
1978	1.75	.80
1979	3.50	1.00
1980	4.75	1.90
1981	3.00	1.15
1982 to date	2.50	1.50

OPINION:

One of the most attractive junior silver mining stocks with a property that is key to the operation of Sunshine. It is a take over candidate by Sunshine.

Midnite
Mines
Inc.

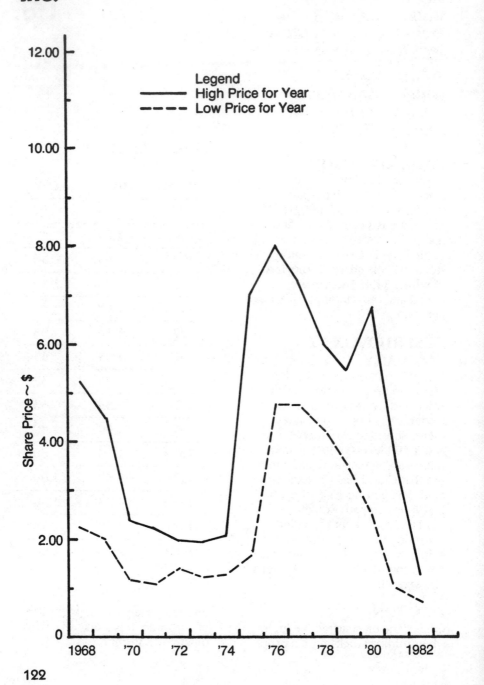

Spokane OTC
Inc. 1954
Washington

Midnite Mines Inc.

14040 N.E. 8th St.
Suite 105, Bldg. C.
Bellevue, WA 98007
Pres. –Thomas E.
    Wynecoop
Sec./Treas. –Robert E.
    Blair

Transfer Agent:
Seattle First National
    Bank
P.O. Box 24186
Seattle, WA 98124

CAPITALIZATION:
Common stock, 10¢ par value, authorized 6,000,000 shares. Issued and outstanding: 4,123,500 shares.

DESCRIPTION OF COMPANY:
Owns 49% of Dawn Mining Co., a Newmont Mining Corp. subsidiary which operates the Midnite uranium mine in the Spokane Indian Reservaton and the Ford, Washington, uranium processing mill. The mine has been a major uranium producer and dividend payer. Also owns and operates the Polaris silver mine near Dillon, Montana. Holds a large block of claims southeast of Mullan, Idaho, near Montana border.

OPINION:
This stock has always been looked upon as a uranium producer even though they have some silver. In its past price

PRICE HISTORY:

YEAR	HIGH	LOW
1968	5.25	2.25
1969	4.50	2.00
1970	2.40	1.20
1971	2.25	1.10
1972	2.00	1.40
1973	1.95	1.25
1974	2.10	1.30
1975	7.00	1.65
1976	8.00	4.75
1977	7.25	4.75
1978	6.00	4.25
1979	5.50	3.50
1980	6.75	2.50
1981	3.50	1.00
1982 to date	1.25	.75

peaks were a reflection of the uranium boom at the time. Interest could come into Midnite again if uranium moves into the forefront and/or investors recognize the silver possibilities in the company.

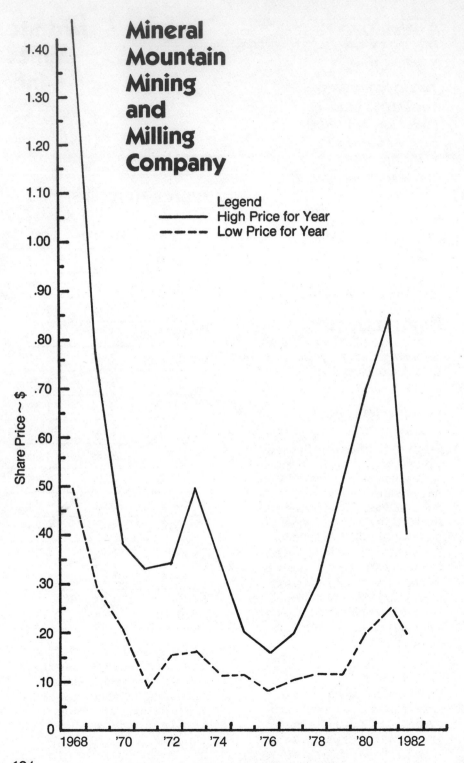

Mineral
Mountain
Mining
and
Milling
Company

Legend
——— High Price for Year
- - - - Low Price for Year

Share Price ~ $

1.40
1.30
1.20
1.10
1.00
.90
.80
.70
.60
.50
.40
.30
.20
.10
0

1968 '70 '72 '74 '76 '78 '80 1982

Spokane Stock Exchange
Inc. 1932
Idaho

17500 E. Wellesley
Spokane, WA 99216
Pres.–M.L. Schwary
Sec.–E.M. Borjessan

Transfer Agent:
17500 E. Wellesley
Spokane, WA 99216

Mineral Mountain Mining and Milling Company

CAPITALIZATION:
Capital stock, common, nonassessable, 5¢ par value, authorized 3,000,000 shares; issued and outstanding, 2,318,736 shares.

DESCRIPTION OF COMPANY:
Owns one-third interest in "Mineral Mountain Area" of CDA District Silver Belt. The area consists of company's original four patented claims and portions of Chester and Polaris properties north of a warped plane lying parallel to and 300 feet northerly from center of Chester vein which has been mined from Sunshine mine workings.

OPINION:
Probably a buy if the silver market continues upward.

PRICE HISTORY:

YEAR	HIGH	LOW
1968	1.45	.50
1969	.78	.29
1970	.38	.21
1971	.33	.09
1972	.34	.15
1973	.49	.16
1974	.34	.11
1975	.20	.11
1976	.16	.08
1977	.20	.10
1978	.30	.11
1979	.50	.11
1980	.70	.20
1981	.85	.25
1982 to date	.40	.20

Nabob
Silver
Lead
Company

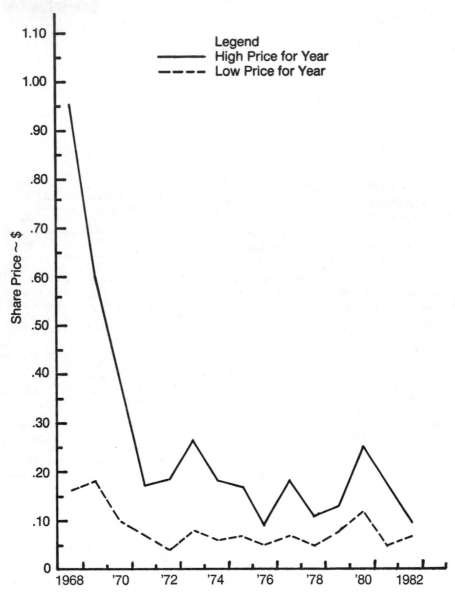

Spokane OTC
Inc. 1923
Idaho

P.O. Box 899
Wallace, ID 83873
Pres. –James B. Colson
Sec. –June Olson

Transfer Agent:
P.O. Box 899
Wallace, ID 83873

Nabob Silver Lead Company

CAPITALIZATION:

Capital stock, par value 25¢ per share; authorized and issued, 3,500,000 shares; 3,302,286 shares outstanding.

DESCRIPTION OF COMPANY:

Owns the Nabob mine, a former zinc-lead-silver producer, in Pine Creek sector, CDA District. Mine company's 42 claims surrounding it leased to Cominco American, Inc., March 1, 1982. The Nabob mill is leased to Robert A. Rice, Silverton, Idaho.

OPINION:

Stock appears very cheap at this writing. Could go substantially higher with a large and continuous move in silver.

PRICE HISTORY:

YEAR	HIGH	LOW
1968	.95	.16
1969	.60	.18
1970	.38	.10
1971	.17	.07
1972	.18	.04
1973	.26	.08
1974	.18	.06
1975	.17	.07
1976	.09	.05
1977	.18	.07
1978	.11	.05
1979	.13	.08
1980	.25	.12
1981	.17	.05
1982 to date	.10	.07

Nancy Lee Mines, Inc.

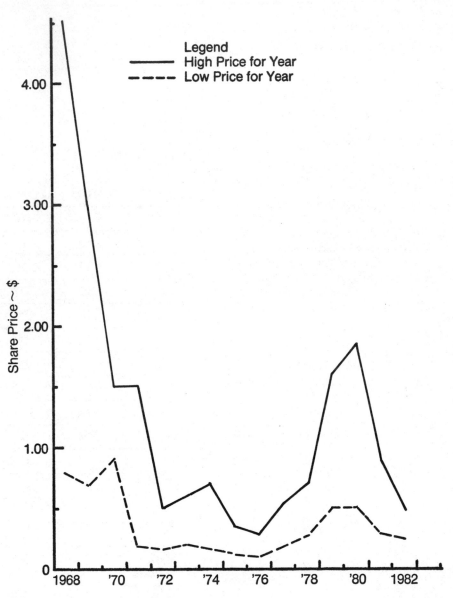

*Spokane OTC
Inc. 1936
Idaho*

*P.O. Box 5397
Spokane, WA 99205
Pres.–William F. Nielsen
Sec.–Phyllis Gaylord*

*Transfer Agent:
Spokane Guaranty Co.
1306 Washington Mutual
   Bldg.
Spokane, WA 99201*

Nancy Lee Mines, Inc.

CAPITALIZATION:
Common stock 25¢ par value, authorized 5,000,000 shares; issued and outstanding, 4,987,564 shares.

DESCRIPTION OF COMPANY:
Owns 436-acre Nancy Lee mine property, Mineral County, Montana, near Superior, and mineral rights to 213 unpatented claims on adjacent leased properties. Past operators mined and milled substantial tonnages of silver-lead-copper-gold-zinc ore. Current lessee has developed new ore reserves and is reorganizing and refinancing to resume operations.

OPINION:
A new operator and higher silver prices could give a substantial boost to the price of Nancy Lee. It could be cheap at this writing.

PRICE HISTORY:

YEAR	HIGH	LOW
1968	4.50	.80
1969	3.00	.70
1970	1.50	.90
1971	1.50	.20
1972	.50	.17
1973	.60	.20
1974	.70	15
1975	.35	.12
1976	.30	.10
1977	.55	.18
1978	.70	.28
1979	1.60	.50
1980	1.85	.50
1981	.90	.30
1982 to date	.48	.25

National Silver Lead Mining Company

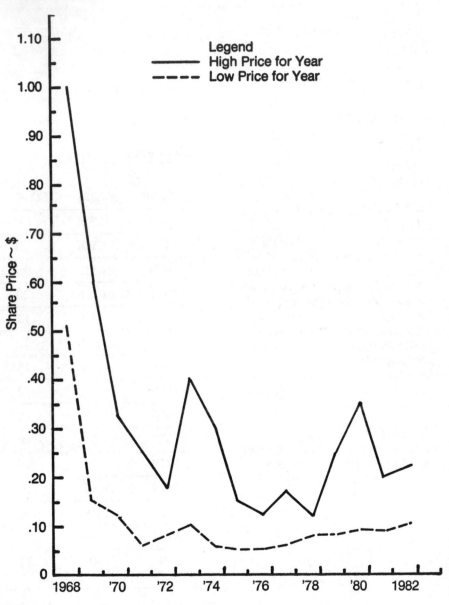

Spokane OTC
Inc. 1906
Idaho

P.O. Box 469
Wallace, ID 83873
Pres. –H.F. Magnuson
Sec. –D.L. Hess

Transfer Agent:
H.F. Magnuson & Co.
P.O. Box 469
Wallace, ID 83873

National Silver Lead Mining Company

CAPITALIZATION:
3,500,000 shares of authorized capital stock with a par value of 10¢ per share. As of December 31, 1981, there were 3,324,623 shares of stock issued and outstanding.

DESCRIPTION OF COMPANY:
The company's business consists of the ownership of mining claims located in Shoshone County, Idaho. The property of the company consists of 39 unpatented and seven patented mining claims about 2 miles south of Sunshine mine. Property bisected by Placer Creek Fault. Exploration work so far limited to near surface.

OPINION:
One of the more interesting penny silver stocks that probably will sell higher with higher silver prices.

PRICE HISTORY:

YEAR	HIGH	LOW
1968	1.00	.50
1969	.60	.15
1970	.32	.12
1971	.25	.06
1972	.18	.08
1973	.40	.10
1974	.30	.06
1975	.15	.05
1976	.12	.05
1977	.17	.06
1978	.12	.08
1979	.25	.08
1980	.35	.09
1981	.20	.08
1982 to date	.22	.10

Nesco
Resources,
Inc.

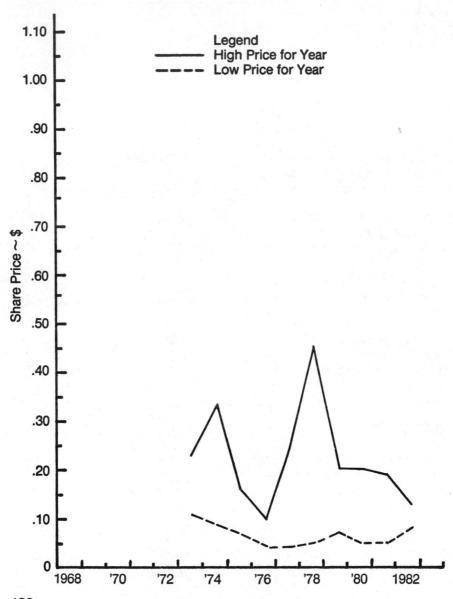

Spokane Stock Exchange Inc. 1968 Washington

1260 Seafirst Financial Center Spokane, WA 99201 Pres. –S. Richard Hansen

Transfer Agent: Spokane Guaranty Co. 1306 Washington Mutual Bank Bldg. Spokane, WA 99201

Nesco Resources, Inc.

CAPITALIZATION:
15,000,000 capital stock authorized, no par value. Issued and outstanding, 7,500,000 shares.

DESCRIPTION OF COMPANY:
Name changed in 1982 from Nesco Mining Corp., organized to acquire a number of early-day silver-gold producers in Colville Indian Reservation, northeastern Washington. Also changed management and now headed by Canadian oil men.

OPINION:
Aggressive new management now makes this stock attractive again. Could do better with a continuous move in silver.

PRICE HISTORY:

YEAR	HIGH	LOW
1973	.23	.11
1974	.33	.09
1975	.16	.07
1976	.10	.04
1977	.24	.04
1978	.45	.05
1979	.20	.07
1980	.20	.05
1981	.19	.05
1982 to date	.13	.08

Nevada Stewart Mining Company

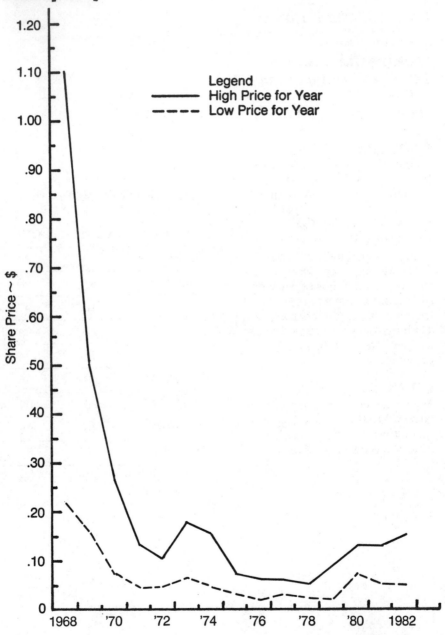

Spokane OTC
Inc. 1915
Idaho

P.O. Box 469
Wallace, ID 83873
Pres. –Tom Smith
Sec. –R. Maurice Cooper

Transfer Agent:
H.F. Magnuson & Co.
P.O. Box 469
Wallace, ID 83873

Nevada Stewart Mining Company

CAPITALIZATION:
4,000,000 shares of authorized capital stock with a par value of 10¢ per share. As of June 30, 1981, there were 2,722,691 shares issued and outstanding.

DESCRIPTION OF COMPANY:
Its six patented and 12 unpatented claims are southwest of Kellogg and border the Bunker Hill, Sidney and Highland-Surprise properties. Partially explored from Highland-Surprise mine shaft years ago. Company doing only required annual assessment work.

OPINION:
Higher silver prices could bring renewed interest into the stock of Nevada Stewart.

PRICE HISTORY:

YEAR	HIGH	LOW
1968	1.10	.22
1969	.50	.15
1970	.26	.07
1971	.13	.04
1972	.10	.04
1973	.17	.06
1974	.15	.04
1975	.07	.03
1976	.06	.02
1977	.06	.03
1978	.05	.02
1979	.09	.02
1980	.13	.07
1981	.13	.05
1982 to date	.15	.05

New
Hilarity
Mining
Company

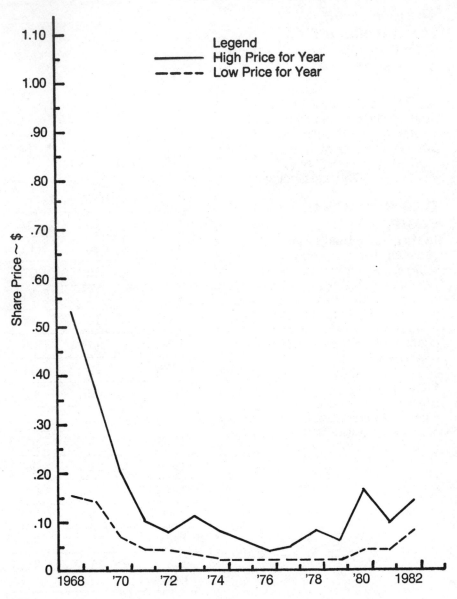

Spokane Stock Exchange
Inc. 1945
Idaho

17500 E. Wellesley
Spokane, WA 99216
Pres. – Wendell Robert
   Brainard
Sec. – E.M. Borjessan

Transfer Agent:
17500 E. Wellesley
Spokane, WA 99216

New Hilarity Mining Company

CAPITALIZATION:

Capital stock: common, nonassessable, 10¢ par value, authorized 3,000,000 shares; issued and outstanding, 3,000,000 shares.

DESCRIPTION OF COMPANY:

Owner of 15 unpatented claims in Pine Creek sector, CDA District. Claims leased to Signal Silver-Gold, which recently signed prospecting agreement with Cominco American, Inc. Owns large blocks of stock in Yreka United and United Mines.

OPINION:

Appears fully priced at this writing, but higher silver prices could bring additional buyers into the stock.

PRICE HISTORY:

YEAR	HIGH	LOW
1968	.53	.15
1969	.37	.14
1970	.20	.07
1971	.10	.04
1972	.08	.04
1973	.11	.03
1974	.08	.02
1975	.06	.02
1976	.04	.02
1977	.05	.02
1978	.08	.02
1979	.06	.02
1980	.16	.04
1981	.10	.04
1982 to date	.14	.08

137

Niagara Mining & Development Company

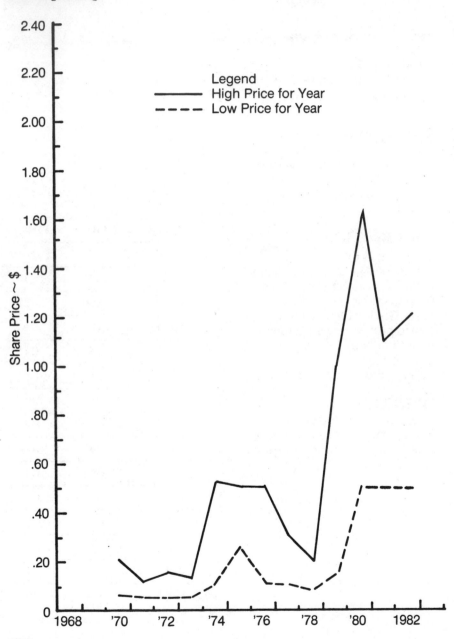

Spokane OTC
Inc. 1955
Idaho

P.O. Box 970
816 Sherman Ave.
Coeur d'Alene, ID 83814
Pres.–Jack Taitch
Sec.–Rita Hamilton

Transfer Agent:
P.O. Box 970
Coeur d'Alene, ID 83814

Niagara Mining & Development Company

CAPITALIZATION:
Common stock, par value 10¢, authorized 3,000,000 shares; issued and outstanding, 1,979,852 shares.

DESCRIPTION OF COMPANY:
Organized to explore 32 claims in old Murray gold camp, CDA District, formerly owned by defunct Blaine and Emmet Mining Co. In 1970 acquired control of Blue Eagle Mining Co., owner of eight claims south of Highland-Surprise in Pine Creek zinc area of CDA District.

OPINION:
Stock appears fully priced at this writing. Could be interesting again on a sharp decline.

PRICE HISTORY:

YEAR	HIGH	LOW
1970	.20	.06
1971	.12	.05
1972	.15	.05
1973	.13	.05
1974	.52	.10
1975	.50	.25
1976	.50	.11
1977	.30	.10
1978	.20	.08
1979	1.00	.15
1980	1.65	.50
1981	1.10	.50
1982 to date	1.20	.50

Oom
Paul
Consolidated
Mining
Company

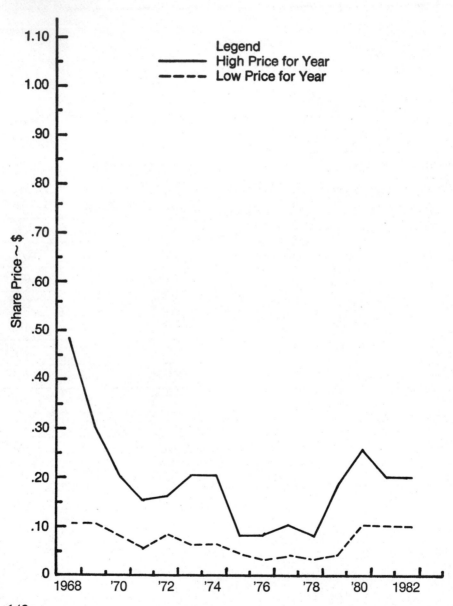

*Spokane OTC
Inc. 1907
Idaho*

*North 2026 Washington
Spokane, WA 99205
(509) 327-5571
Pres. – Charles A. Tilford*

*Transfer Agent:
c/o LeMasters & Daniels
212 Symons Bldg.
Spokane, WA 99204*

Oom Paul Consolidated Mining Company

CAPITALIZATION:
Common stock, par value $1;
1,600,000 shares authorized and
1,600,000 shares issued;
481,699 are held as treasury
stock.

DESCRIPTION OF COMPANY:
Owns 10 patented mining claims
northeast of Burke. No exploration work done in recent years.
Has more than $100,000 in net
current assets, mostly from
timber sales and investments in
U.S. Treasury Bills.

OPINION:
Stock could be a "sleeper."
Would obviously go higher on
any big increase in price of
silver.

PRICE HISTORY:

YEAR	HIGH	LOW
1968	.48	.10
1969	.30	.10
1970	.20	.08
1971	.15	.05
1972	.16	.08
1973	.20	.06
1974	.20	.06
1975	.08	.04
1976	.08	.03
1977	.10	.04
1978	.08	.03
1979	.18	.04
1980	.25	.10
1981	.20	.10
1982 to date	.20	.10

Placer Creek Mining Company

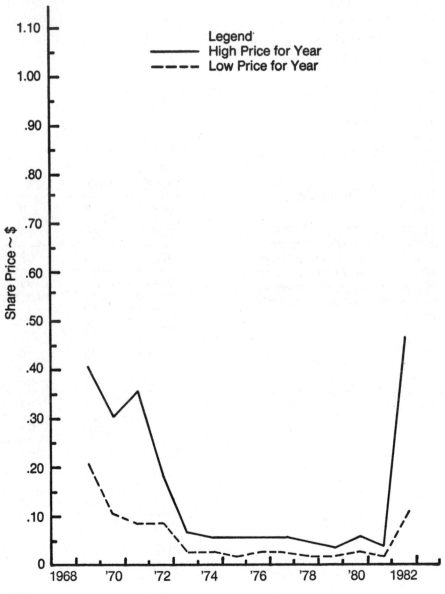

Spokane OTC
Inc. 1967
Idaho

P.O. Box 469
Wallace, ID 83873
Pres. – Walter L. Sly
Sec. – D.L. Hess

Transfer Agent:
H.F. Magnuson & Co.
P.O. Box 469
Wallace, ID 83873

Placer Creek Mining Company

CAPITALIZATION:
6,000,000 shares of authorized nonassessable, capital stock with a par value of 10¢ per share; 5,932,581 shares of stock issued and outstanding.

DESCRIPTION OF COMPANY:
Holds 104 mining claims south and southwest of Wallace, stretching for several miles along the Placer Creek Fault. Company has done geological work, soil sampling and some tunneling. Area relatively unexplored. In September, 1982, it was announced that Bear Creek Mining Co. (Kennecott-owned) had leased the claims and then assigned them to Anaconda Minerals Co. (Atlantic Richfield-owned) for exploration.

OPINION:
Investors' interest will probably increase when Atlantic Richfield interest in Placer Creek becomes more widely known.

PRICE HISTORY:

YEAR	HIGH	LOW
1969	.40	.20
1970	.30	.10
1971	.35	.08
1972	.18	.08
1973	.06	.02
1974	.05	.02
1975	.05	.01
1976	.05	.02
1977	.05	.02
1978	.04	.01
1979	.03	.01
1980	.05	.02
1981	.03	.01
1982 to date	.46	.10

143

Plainview Mining Company

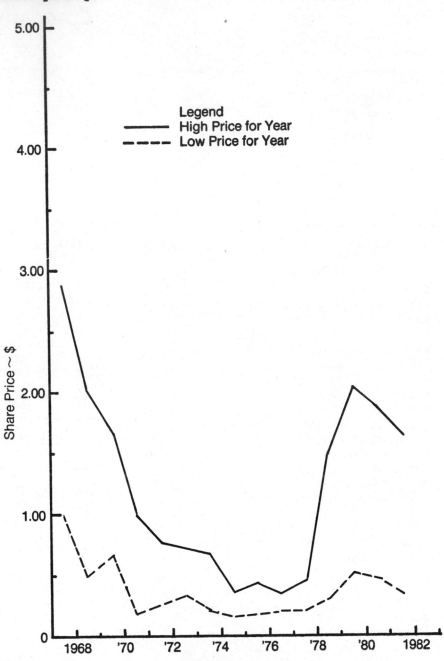

Spokane OTC
Inc. 1927
Idaho

P.O. Box 447
Kellogg, ID 83837
Pres. –Dennis B. Hague
Sec./Treas. –Ronald E.
  Eggart

Transfer Agent:
P.O. Box 447
Kellogg, ID 83837

Plainview Mining Company

CAPITALIZATION:
Capital stock authorized 1,500,000 shares with a par value of 10¢ per share, all of which have been issued.

DESCRIPTION OF COMPANY:
Seven claims south of Osburn in Silver Belt, CDA District. In 1967 unitized with Coeur d'Alene Mines claims adjoining it on south and with northern group of Merger Mines claims into CAMP area. ASARCO undertook to explore CAMP from nearby Coeur d'Alene Mines shaft but abandoned project in 1971 after driving 3500-foot tunnel to target area but before doing planned diamond drilling there. CAMP ground below 900 feet below sea level turned into Consolidated Silver Corp. for stock. CDA Mines undertook exploration of upper CAMP area in 1978 and has driven a 2,000-foot tunnel at creek level.

OPINION:
One of the more interesting and quality penny silver stocks that is closely held. Higher silver prices

PRICE HISTORY:

YEAR	HIGH	LOW
1968	2.85	1.00
1969	2.00	.50
1970	1.65	.65
1971	1.00	.18
1972	.75	.25
1973	.70	.32
1974	.65	.20
1975	.35	.15
1976	.42	.16
1977	.35	.19
1978	.45	.20
1979	1.50	.30
1980	2.00	.50
1981	.85	.45
1982 to date	.65	.35

could cause Plainview stock to move up rather rapidly.

Princeton Mining Company

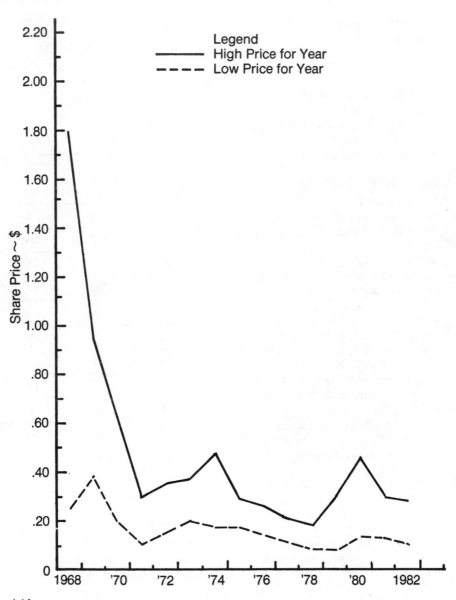

Spokane Stock Exchange
Inc. 1950
Idaho

413 Cedar St.
Wallace, ID 83873
Pres. –R.J. Bruning
Sec. –D.L. Hess

Transfer Agent:
413 Cedar St.
Wallace, ID 83873

Princeton Mining Company

CAPITALIZATION:
Capital stock, par value 10¢ per share, authorized 3,000,000 shares, all of which are issued and outstanding.

DESCRIPTION OF COMPANY:
Holds 40 unpatented claims about 3 miles east of Hecla's Lucky Friday mine. Under a 1962 agreement, Magna Mining Co., Portland, Oregon, drove 500-foot adit which intersected mineral-bearing veins, sank 200-foot shaft and did other work which earned it a 60% deed interest in the claims.

OPINION:
In previous active markets has been a popular listed penny silver stock.

PRICE HISTORY:

YEAR	HIGH	LOW
1968	1.80	.25
1969	.94	.38
1970	.62	.19
1971	.30	.10
1972	.35	.15
1973	.37	.19
1974	.47	.17
1975	.29	.17
1976	.26	.14
1977	.21	.11
1978	.18	.08
1979	.30	.08
1980	.45	.13
1981	.30	.13
1982 to date	.28	.10

Rock
Creek
Mining
Company

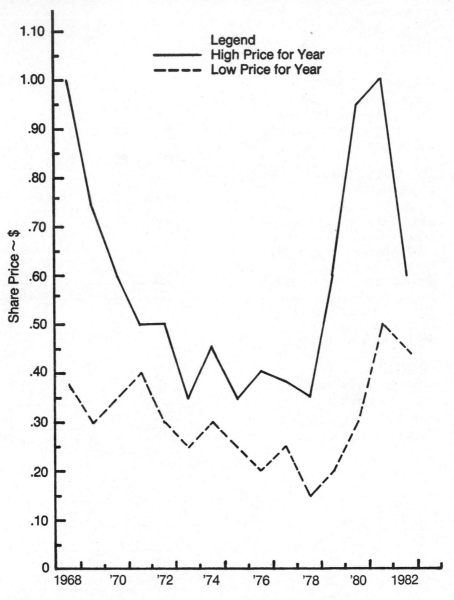

Legend
— High Price for Year
--- Low Price for Year

Share Price ~ $

1.10
1.00
.90
.80
.70
.60
.50
.40
.30
.20
.10
0

1968   '70   '72   '74   '76   '78   '80   1982

Spokane OTC
Inc. 1947
Idaho

P.O. Box 469
Wallace, ID 83873
Pres. –H.F. Magnuson
Sec. –D.L. Hess

Transfer Agent:
H.F. Magnuson & Co.
P.O. Box 469
Wallace, ID 83873

Rock Creek Mining Company

CAPITALIZATION:
6,000,000 shares of authorized nonassessable, capital stock with a par value of 10¢ per share. As of December 31, 1981, there were 5,924,400 shares of stock issued and outstanding.

DESCRIPTION OF COMPANY:
Owns big block of 175 claims east of Wallace and adjoining the Silver Buckle property. Rock Creek ground penetrated by a 4,800-foot tunnel driven from Gem State property by Hecla years ago. In the spring of 1982 Teck Resources (U.S.) Inc. entered into an agreement to explore the combined areas of 215 claims.

OPINION:
One of the better quality penny stocks in the CDA Silver Mining Region because of Teck Resources interest in exploring this property. Stock could attract further buying on any news coming out of Teck Resources' exploration.

PRICE HISTORY:

YEAR	HIGH	LOW
1968	1.00	.38
1969	.75	.30
1970	.60	.35
1971	.50	.40
1972	.50	.30
1973	.35	.25
1974	.45	.30
1975	.35	.25
1976	.40	.20
1977	.38	.25
1978	.35	.15
1979	.60	.20
1980	.95	.30
1981	1.00	.50
1982 to date	.60	.45

149

Royal
Apex
Silver,
Inc.

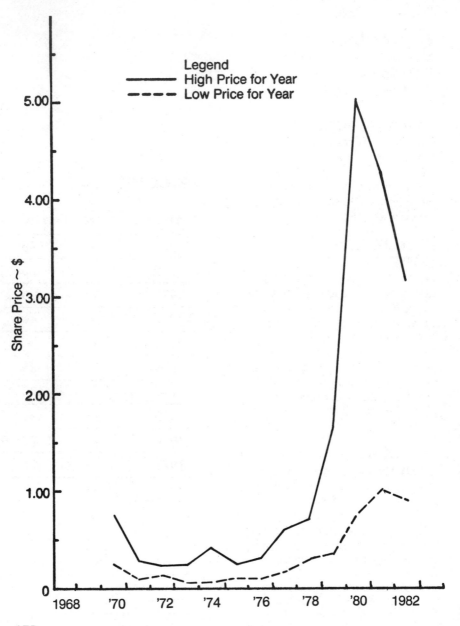

Spokane OTC
Inc. 1965
Idaho

412 River St.
Wallace, ID 83873
(509) 556-1529
Pres. –Justin L. Rice
Sec. –David E.P. Lindh

Transfer Agent:
P.O. Box 886
Wallace, ID 83873

Royal Apex Silver, Inc.

CAPITALIZATION:
20,000,000 shares of nonassessable common stock of a par value of 5¢ each, of which 11,439,366 shares were issued and outstanding.

DESCRIPTION OF COMPANY:
Its 90-claim Harlow silver prospect 2 miles north of Osburn, Idaho, is being explored by Coeur d'Alene Mines Corp., which in 1982 exercised a stock option to acquire 5,696,961 shares (49.8%) of Royal Apex. The latter acquired 1 million shares (16.6%) of CDA Mines in the deal. Royal Apex's Silver State property in Nevada is leased to ASARCO, which is conducting a production, feasibility study. Royal Apex has been sampling and mapping the Moose Creek silver-gold property in Montana, acquired in 1980.

OPINION:
Decidedly one of the better quality CDA silver mining stocks that could have long term potential.

PRICE HISTORY:

YEAR	HIGH	LOW
1970	.75	.25
1971	.30	.10
1972	.24	.14
1973	.25	.06
1974	.41	.07
1975	.25	.10
1976	.30	.10
1977	.60	.17
1978	.70	.30
1979	1.65	.35
1980	5.00	.75
1981	4.25	1.00
1982 to date	3.15	.90

Saint Elmo Mining Company

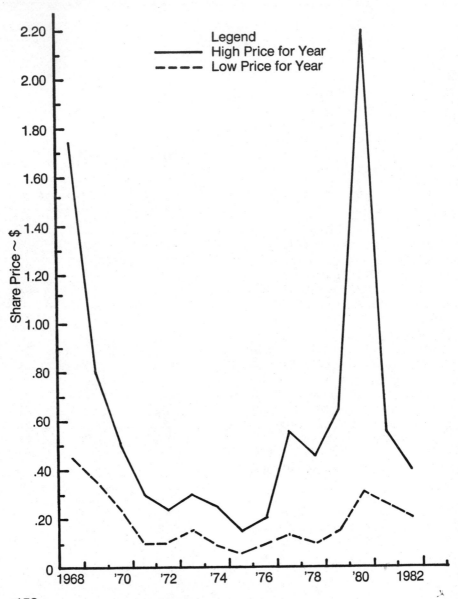

Spokane OTC
Inc. 1935
Idaho

P.O. Box 469
Wallace, ID 83873
Pres. —Robert Weninger
Sec. —D.L. Hess

Transfer Agent:
H.F. Magnuson & Co.
P.O. Box 469
Wallace, ID 83873

Saint Elmo Mining Company

CAPITALIZATION:

2,500,000 shares of authorized nonassessable, capital stock with a par value of 10¢ per share. As of December 31, 1981 there were 1,987,140 shares of stock issued standing.

DESCRIPTION OF COMPANY:

Patented St. Elmo claim south of Osburn, DCA District, Silver Belt. Had some early-day production from shallow workings. Rehabilitation started in 1967 with financing by Silver Dollar Mining Co. (now Sunshine).

OPINION:

Has been a good performer in past markets and because of its small capitalization and the excellent location of its property, stock could again sell up to its old high on higher silver prices.

PRICE HISTORY:

YEAR	HIGH	LOW
1968	1.75	.55
1969	.80	.35
1970	.50	.24
1971	.30	.10
1972	.24	.10
1973	.30	.15
1974	.25	.09
1975	.15	.06
1976	.20	.10
1977	.55	.13
1978	.45	.10
1979	.65	.15
1980	2.20	.30
1981	.55	.25
1982 to date	.40	.20

153

Shoshone Silver Mining Company

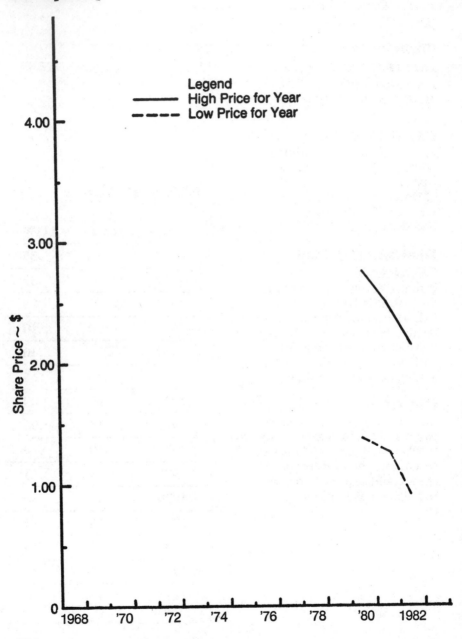

Spokane OTC
Inc. 1969
Idaho

P.O. Box 2011
Coeur d'Alene, ID 83814
Pres. –Irvin Scheller

Transfer Agent:
P.O. Box 2011
Coeur d'Alene, ID 83814

Shoshone Silver Mining Company

CAPITALIZATION:
Common stock, 10¢ par value, authorized 5,000,000 shares. Issued and outstanding, 4,914,747 shares.

DESCRIPTION OF COMPANY:
Owns five patented and 70 unpatented claims southeast of Mullan, Idaho, adjacent to the Montana border, which are being explored by Bear Creek Mining Co. (exploration subsidiary of Kennecott Corp.) under agreements signed late in 1981. Shoshone is continuing exploration of the leased Weber, Keep Kool and Idaho Lakeview near the southern end of Lake Pend Oreille. All are former producers. Also has an interest in an operating agreement on Belleville Group in Bonner County. Owns seven claims on Hall Mountain, Boundary County.

OPINION:
Stock appears fully priced at this time.

PRICE HISTORY:

YEAR	HIGH	LOW
1980	2.75	1.35
1981	2.50	1.25
1982 to date	2.15	.85

Sidney Mining Company

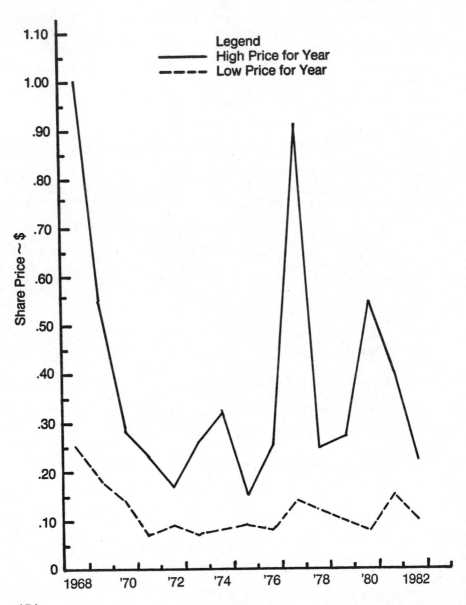

*Spokane Stock Exchange
Inc. 1910
Idaho*

*123 McKinley Ave.
Kellogg, ID 83837
Pres. –M.C. Brown
Sec. –Ben Smick*

*Transfer Agent:
P.O. Box 1049
Kellogg, ID 83837*

Sidney Mining Company

CAPITALIZATION:
8,000,000 shares authorized at 10¢ par value, of which 5,429,245 are issued and outstanding.

DESCRIPTION OF COMPANY:
Sidney mine southwest of Kellogg, Idaho, yielded $32 million in zinc-lead-silver before shut down in 1959 as worked out. However, Cominco American recently leased the property under a prospecting agreement. Sidney's St. Paul–Snowshoe properties near Libby, Montana, under lease-option agreement with Lincoln Resources, U.S. subsidiary of Greenwood Explorations, Inc., Vancouver, B.C. Negotiations under way for operator of Sidney's Silver City, Idaho, property.

OPINION:
Could again become more active in any general move in silver.

PRICE HISTORY:

YEAR	HIGH	LOW
1968	1.00	.25
1969	.55	.18
1970	.28	.14
1971	.23	.07
1972	.17	.09
1973	.26	.07
1974	.32	.08
1975	.15	.09
1976	.25	.08
1977	.91	.14
1978	.25	.12
1979	.27	.10
1980	.55	.08
1981	.40	.15
1982 to date	.22	.10

Signal Silver & Gold, Inc.

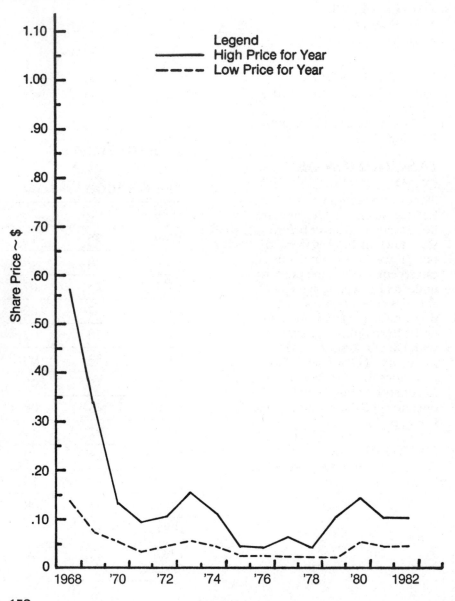

Spokane OTC
Inc. 1906
Idaho

P.O. Box 668
Coeur d'Alene, ID 83814
Pres. – Stanley Harrison

Transfer Agent:
c/o Consolidated Metals
P.O. Box 668
Coeur d'Alene, ID 83813

Signal Silver & Gold, Inc.

CAPITALIZATION:
Capital stock, authorized 10,000,000 shares of nonassessable common stock with a par value of 25¢ per share, 4,449,644 of which have been issued and are outstanding.

DESCRIPTION OF COMPANY:
Its holdings include two patented and 10 unpatented claims adjacent to Mascot Silver-Lead Mines in the Pine Creek sector of the CDA District and 17 unpatented claims about 4 miles south of Wallace. The Pine Creek property was leased by Cominco American in 1979.

OPINION:
None.

PRICE HISTORY:

YEAR	HIGH	LOW
1968	.57	.13
1969	.33	.07
1970	.13	.05
1971	.09	.03
1972	.10	.04
1973	.15	.05
1974	.11	.04
1975	.04	.02
1976	.04	.02
1977	.06	.02
1978	.04	.02
1979	.10	.02
1980	.14	.05
1981	.10	.04
1982 to date	.10	.04

Silver Beaver Mining Company, Inc.

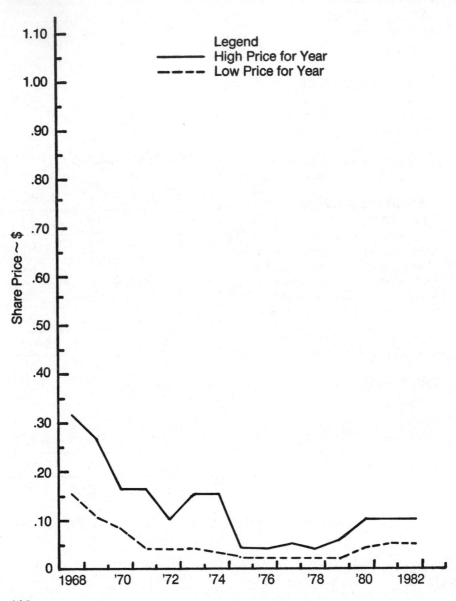

Spokane OTC
Inc. 1967
Idaho

P.O. Box 1127
Wallace, ID 83873
(208) 753-9562
Pres. –Frank Morbeck
Sec. –Wesley G. Bailey

Transfer Agent:
504 Bank St.
P.O. Box 1127
Wallace, ID 83873

Silver Beaver Mining Company, Inc.

CAPITALIZATION:
Capital stock nonassessable 10¢ par value per share; 5,000,000 authorized; 2,958,540 shares issued and outstanding.

DESCRIPTION OF COMPANY:
Silver Beaver Mining Company owns 58 unpatented mining claims in the Beaver Mining District, 8 miles north of Wallace, Idaho. It also owns 18 unpatented mining claims in the Jack White Mining District. The company has through the years done annual assessment work and some development work on these properties.

OPINION:
None.

PRICE HISTORY:

YEAR	HIGH	LOW
1968	.31	.15
1969	.26	.10
1970	.16	.08
1971	.16	.04
1972	.10	.04
1973	.15	.04
1974	.15	.03
1975	.04	.02
1976	.04	.02
1977	.05	.02
1978	.04	.02
1979	.06	.02
1980	.10	.04
1981	.10	.05
1982 to date	.10	.05

Silver Belt Mines, Inc.

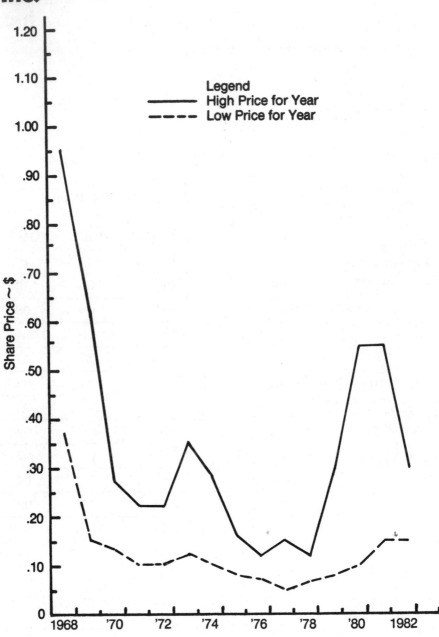

Spokane OTC
Inc. 1947
Idaho

P.O. Box 469
Wallace, ID 83873
Pres.–H.F. Magnuson
Sec.–D.L. Hess

Transfer Agent:
H.F. Magnuson & Co.
P.O. Box 469
Wallace, ID 83873

Silver Belt Mines, Inc.

CAPITALIZATION:
3,500,000 shares of authorized nonassessable, capital stock with a par value of 10¢ per share. As of December 31, 1981, there were 1,671,073 shares of stock issued and outstanding.

DESCRIPTION OF COMPANY:
Has 32 mining claims in CDA District some of which border ground of Bunker Hill and the Sun Con property of Sunshine Mining Co. Claims relatively unexplored for lack of adequate finances.

OPINION:
On a major move in silver the stock could be attractive.

PRICE HISTORY:

YEAR	HIGH	LOW
1968	.95	.37
1969	.62	.15
1970	.27	.13
1971	.22	.10
1972	.22	.10
1973	.35	.12
1974	.28	.10
1975	.16	.08
1976	.12	.07
1977	.15	.05
1978	.12	.07
1979	.30	.08
1980	.55	.10
1981	.55	.15
1982 to date	.30	.15

163

Silver Bowl, Inc.

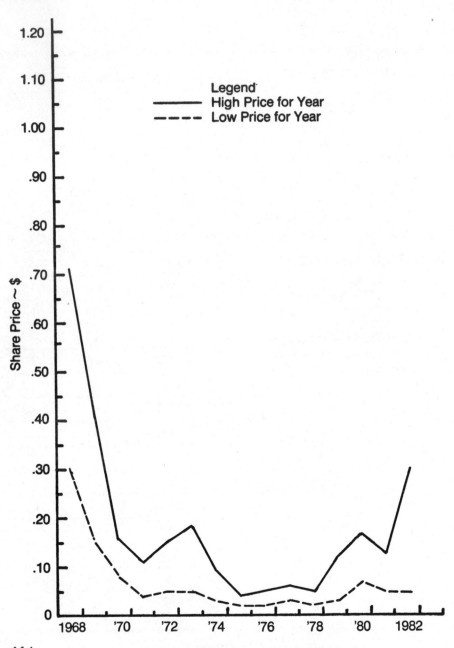

Spokane OTC
Inc. 1930
Idaho

Silver Bowl, Inc.

P.O. Box 668
Coeur d'Alene, ID 83814
Pres.–Stanley Harrison
Sec.–Frank Morbeck

Transfer Agent:
P.O. Box 668
Coeur d'Alene, ID 83814

CAPITALIZATION:

Capital stock: authorized
10,000,000 shares of nonassessable common stock with a par
value of 25¢ per share,
9,866,639 shares of which are
issued.

DESCRIPTION OF COMPANY:

Acquired 300 claims several
miles south of Sunshine mine,
CDA District, as surviving firm of
a 1965 merger of Silver Bowl,
Coeur d'Alene Giant, Allied Silver and Silver Pirate properties.

OPINION:

Has one of the larger properties
in the CDA Silver Mining District, just south of the Sunshine
mine. This and the start of a
major move in silver has brought
interest into the stock.

PRICE HISTORY:

YEAR	HIGH	LOW
1968	.71	.30
1969	.40	.15
1970	.16	.08
1971	.11	.04
1972	.10	.05
1973	.18	.05
1974	.09	.03
1975	.04	.02
1976	.05	.02
1977	.06	.03
1978	.05	.02
1979	.12	.03
1980	.17	.07
1981	.13	.05
1982 to date	.30	.05

Silver Buckle Mining Company

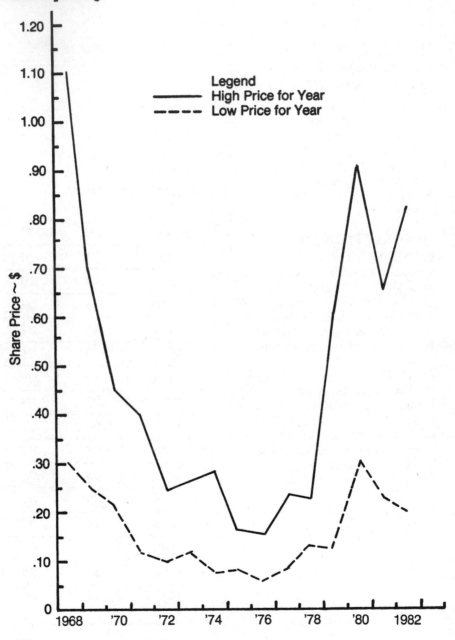

Legend
—— High Price for Year
---- Low Price for Year

Share Price ~ $

1.20
1.10
1.00
.90
.80
.70
.60
.50
.40
.30
.20
.10
0

1968 '70 '72 '74 '76 '78 '80 1982

Spokane OTC
Inc. 1962
Idaho

Silver Buckle Mining Company

P.O. Box 1088
Wallace, ID 83873
Pres. – Wray Featherstone
Sec. –D.L. Hess

Transfer Agent:
P.O. Box 1088
Wallace, ID 83873

CAPITALIZATION:
12,000,000 shares of authorized, capital stock, par value 10¢; 11,838,155 shares issued and outstanding.

DESCRIPTION OF COMPANY:
Controls about 3,000 acres on the three sides of Wallace in CDA District, including block just north of Callahan Mining Co.'s Galena mine. Owns 918,847 shares of Vindicator Silver-Lead Mining Company capital stock. Signed an exploration agreement with Anaconda Mineral Co., a division of Atlantic Richfield Co., announced in September, 1982.

OPINION:
In view of the recent joint venture between Silver Buckle and Anaconda, a division of Atlantic Richfield, I would rate the stock one of the more attractive of the low priced Coeur d'Alene silver stocks.

PRICE HISTORY:

YEAR	HIGH	LOW
1968	1.10	.30
1969	.70	.25
1970	.45	.21
1971	.40	.12
1972	.24	.10
1973	.26	.12
1974	.28	.08
1975	.16	.08
1976	.15	.06
1977	.23	.08
1978	.22	.12
1979	.60	.12
1980	.90	.30
1981	.65	.23
1982 to date	.82	.20

167

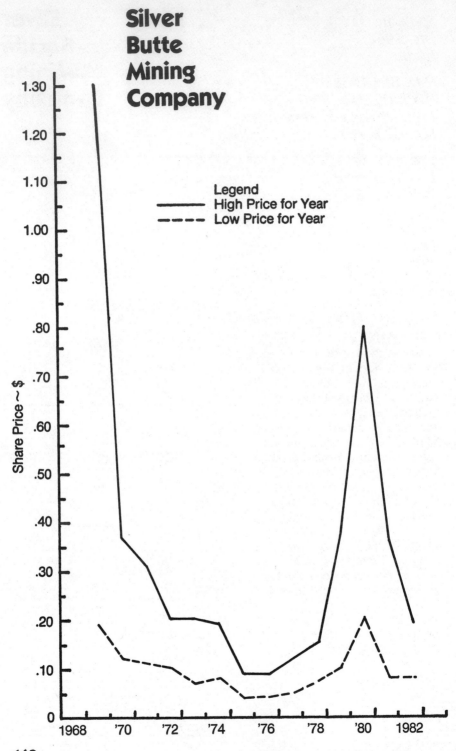

Silver Butte Mining Company

Legend
— High Price for Year
---- Low Price for Year

Share Price ~ $

Spokane Stock Exchange Inc. 1965
Idaho

P.O. Box 711
Sandpoint, ID 83864
Pres.—Cliff Hohman
Sec./Treas.—Harlow
  McConnaughty

Transfer Agent:
P.O. Box 711
Sandpoint, ID 83864

Silver Butte Mining Company

CAPITALIZATION:
Common stock, 5¢ par value,
10,000,000 authorized,
7,513,232 shares issued and
outstanding.

DESCRIPTION OF COMPANY:
Has mineral rights to 11 patented
and 98 unpatented claims and
200-acre state lease on west side
of Idaho's Lake Pend Oreille, including old Talache mine, a substantial early-day silver producer. Company has done considerable exploration, and some
drilling and tunneling has been
done by lessees. Management recently contracted for rehabilitation of a tunnel from which
hand-sorted high grade ore
shipped in 1960s.

OPINION:
Is probably fully priced now.
Tends to move with the other
penny silver stocks on an up-
trend in silver.

PRICE HISTORY:

YEAR	HIGH	LOW
1969	1.30	.19
1970	.37	.12
1971	.31	.11
1972	.20	.10
1973	.20	.07
1974	.19	.08
1975	.09	.04
1976	.09	.04
1977	.12	.05
1978	.15	.07
1979	.37	.10
1980	.80	.20
1981	.36	.08
1982 to date	.19	.08

Silver Cable Mining Company

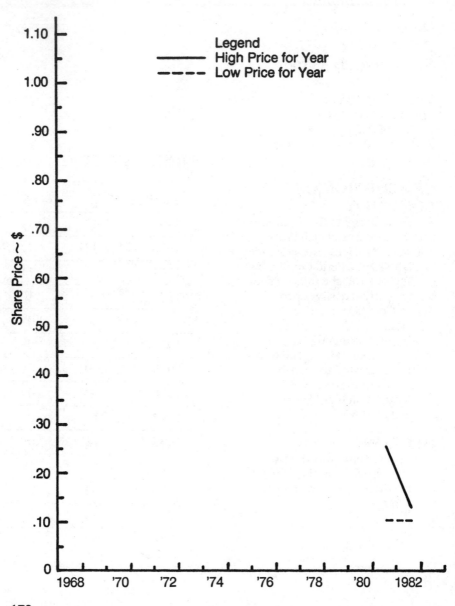

Legend
—— High Price for Year
---- Low Price for Year

Share Price ~ $

1.10
1.00
.90
.80
.70
.60
.50
.40
.30
.20
.10
0

1968 '70 '72 '74 '76 '78 '80 1982

Spokane OTC
Inc. 1934
Montana

P.O. Box 1127
Wallace, ID 83873
(208) 753-9562
Pres. –Frank Morbeck
Sec./Treas. –Virginia
*   Mattern*

Transfer Agent:
P.O. Box 1127
Wallace, ID 83873

Silver Cable Mining Company

CAPITALIZATION:
Capital stock: authorized
2,500,000 shares at 10¢ per
share; 1,901,640 issued and
outstanding.

DESCRIPTION OF COMPANY:
Owns eight patented claims con-
taining old Silver Cable mine on
Montana side of the border east
of Mullan, Idaho. Under Hecla's
operation in World War II the
mine yielded about $550,000
worth of lead-zinc-silver ore.
Idle from 1946 to 1976 when
new management began reopen-
ing old workings and estimating
ore reserves.

OPINION:
None.

PRICE HISTORY:

YEAR	HIGH	LOW
1981	.25	.10
1982 to date	.13	.10

Silver
Crescent,
Inc.

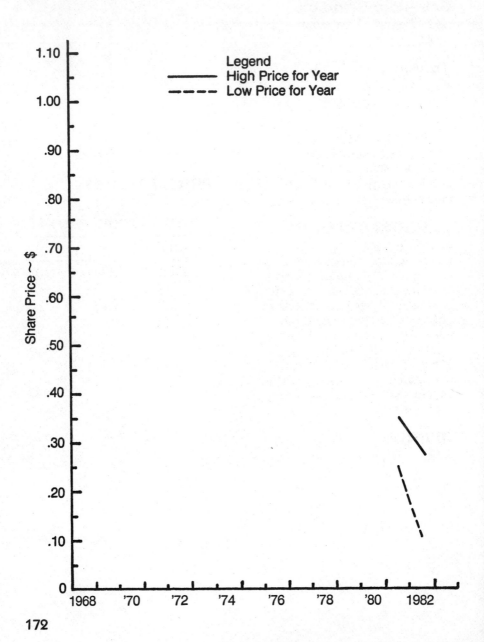

Spokane Stock Exchange Inc. 1890 Idaho

Silver Crescent, Inc.

17500 East Wellesley Ave. Spokane, WA 99216 Pres.–Forrest Garrett Sec.–E.M. Borjessan

Transfer Agent: 17500 East Wellesley Ave. Spokane, WA 99216

CAPITALIZATION:
Capital stock, par value 10¢ per share, of which 1,780,000 were outstanding on December 31, 1981.

DESCRIPTION OF COMPANY:
Holding 113 unpatented claims and mill site northeast of Kellogg, Idaho, and adjoining Capitol Silver and Highland Aurora properties. Company undertaking exploration program on claims recently added to the group. Also owns large block of Silver Bowl stock.

OPINION:
None.

PRICE HISTORY:

YEAR	HIGH	LOW
1981	.35	.25
1982 to date	.28	.11

Silver Crest Mines, Inc.

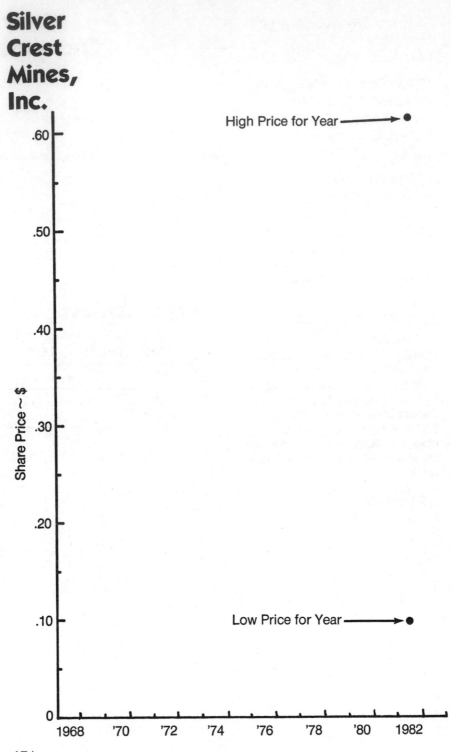

High Price for Year ●

.60
.50
.40
.30
.20
.10
0

Share Price ~ $

Low Price for Year ●

1968 '70 '72 '74 '76 '78 '80 1982

Spokane OTC
Inc. 1968
Idaho

Scott Building
Wallace, ID 83873
Pres. –Irvin Scheller
Sec./Treas.–R.M. MacPhee

Transfer Agent:
H.F. Magnuson & Co.
P.O. Box 469
Wallace, ID 83873

Silver Crest Mines, Inc.

CAPITALIZATION:
Authorized capital of 5,000,000 shares of common nonasessable, 10¢ par stock. Subsequently increased to 10,000,000 shares of which 6,323,033 shares are outstanding.

DESCRIPTION OF COMPANY:
Holds 125 unpatented mining claims southeast of Mullan, Idaho, partly in Shoshone County, Idaho, but mostly across the Idaho-Montana border in Mineral County, Montana, as the result of a 1982 merger of Border Silver Mines, Inc. Bear Creek Mining Co., exploration division of Kennecott Corp., leased the claims late in 1981. In August, 1982, Anaconda Minerals Co., a division of Atlantic Richfield Co., began exploratory drilling under an assignment from Bear Creek.

OPINION:
Is a newly traded stock that is unseasoned in these markets but has attractive properties.

PRICE HISTORY:

YEAR	HIGH	LOW
1982 to date	.62	.10

175

Silver Crystal Mines, Inc.

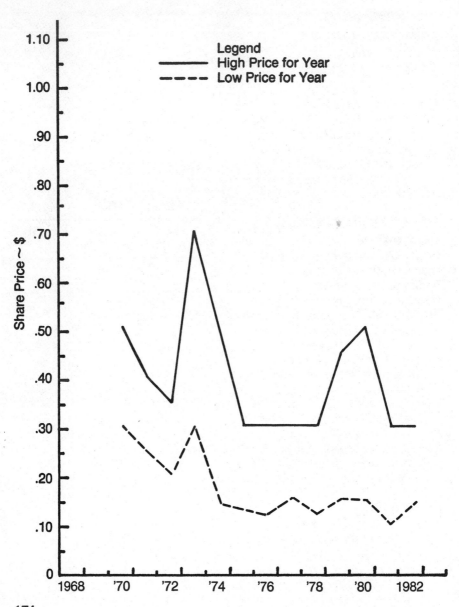

Spokane OTC
Inc. 1968
Idaho

Shoshone Building
Wallace, ID 83873
Pres. – Gene F. Covey

Transfer Agent:
Shoshone Building
Wallace, ID 83873

Silver Crystal Mines, Inc.

CAPITALIZATION:
Common stock, par value 10¢ per share; 5,000,000 shares authorized, 2,551,770 shares issued and outstanding.

DESCRIPTION OF COMPANY:
Holds 12 unpatented claims near Murray, Idaho, which it had been exploring by tunnel work along with mining lead-silver ore from adjacent old Bear Top mine leased from Merger Mines. Ore sales from August 28, 1968, to September 30, 1981 totaled $110,787.

OPINION:
Is a working mine which makes it one of the more potential penny silver stocks.

PRICE HISTORY:

YEAR	HIGH	LOW
1970	.50	.30
1971	.40	.25
1972	.35	.20
1973	.70	.30
1974	.50	.14
1975	.30	.13
1976	.30	.12
1977	.30	.15
1978	.30	.12
1979	.45	.15
1980	.50	.15
1981	.30	.10
1982 to date	.30	.14

177

Silver Hill Mines, Inc.

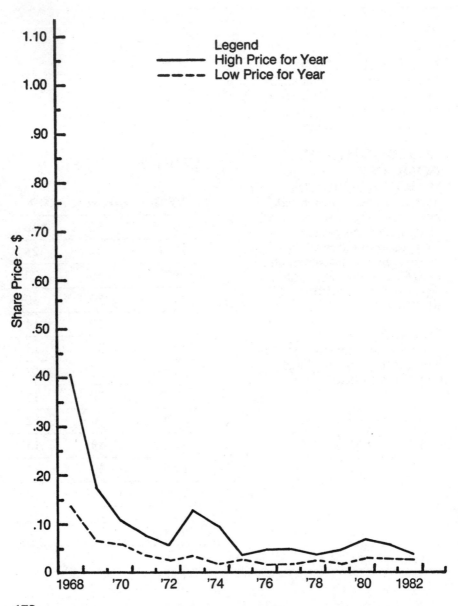

Spokane OTC
Inc. 1961
Idaho

East 10903 Mallon
Spokane, WA 99201
Pres. –Robert C.
* Gillingham*
Sec. –R.M. Swanson

Transfer Agent:
3803 E. 11th Ave.
Spokane, WA 99202

CAPITALIZATION:
Capital stock: 10,000,000 shares authorized; 8,155,288 shares issued and outstanding.

DESCRIPTION OF COMPANY:
Owns 20% undivided interest in 130 acres of deeded land 5 miles south of Spokane, site of an old tin-tungsten mine from which some small shipments were made years ago; a 4% royalty interest in 28 claims northeast of Osburn, Idaho, transferred to Champion Gold & Silver for stock (10,000 shares), and seven claims in Montana leased to Nancy Lee Mines.

OPINION:
None.

PRICE HISTORY:

YEAR	HIGH	LOW
1968	.40	.13
1969	.17	.06
1970	.10	.05
1971	.07	.03
1972	.05	.02
1973	.12	.03
1974	.09	.01
1975	.03	.02
1976	.04	.01
1977	.04	.01
1978	.03	.02
1979	.04	.01
1980	.06	.02
1981	.05	.02
1982 to date	.03	.02

Silver King Mines

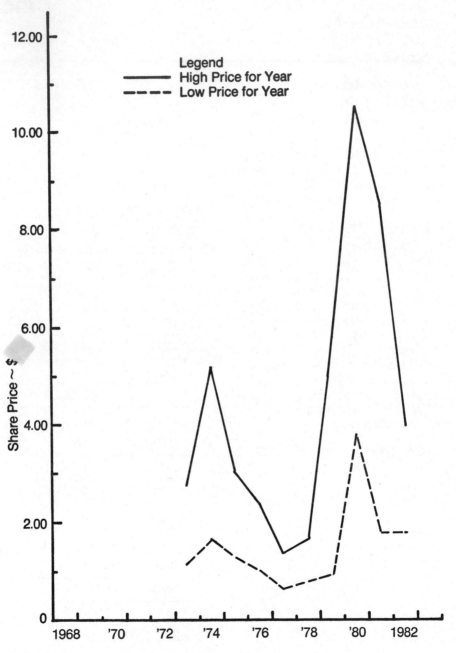

Legend
— High Price for Year
--- Low Price for Year

Share Price ~ $

12.00
10.00
8.00
6.00
4.00
2.00
0

1968   '70   '72   '74   '76   '78   '80   1982

NASDAQ OTC
Inc. 1962
Nevada

322 First Security Bank
 Bldg.
405 S. Main St.
Salt Lake City, UT 84111
(801) 521-3827
Pres. –K.L. Stoker
Sec./Treas. –M.J. Rapp

Transfer Agent:
322 First Security Bank
 Bldg.
405 S. Main St.
Salt Lake City, UT 84111

Silver King Mines

CAPITALIZATION:
Common stock 12,072,215 shares at $1 par value.

DESCRIPTION OF COMPANY:
Silver King owns and operates mining claims known as the Copper Cliff properties in the Seven Devils mining district of Idaho, where an 800-ton-a-day flotation mill is situated. Production from the properties averages about 150,000 pounds of copper and 3,500 ounces of silver monthly. The company also has interests in or manages other properties in the western U.S. The Taylor silver properties located near Ely, Nevada, are now in full production and are expected to yield approximately 1 million ounces of silver bullion annually. Silver King's total net production of silver is 47,500 ounces/year and are thought to have reserves for approximately 20 years.

PRICE HISTORY:

YEAR	HIGH	LOW
1973	2¾	1⅛
1974	5⅛	1⅝
1975	3	1¼
1976	2⅜	1
1977	1⅜	⅝
1978	1⅞	¾
1979	5	⅞
1980	10½	3¾
1981	8½	1¾
1982 to date	3¹⁵⁄₁₆	1¾

OPINION:
This stock has had good performance in past active silver markets. It is looked upon as one of the better quality silver stocks available.

Silver
King
Mining &
Milling
Company

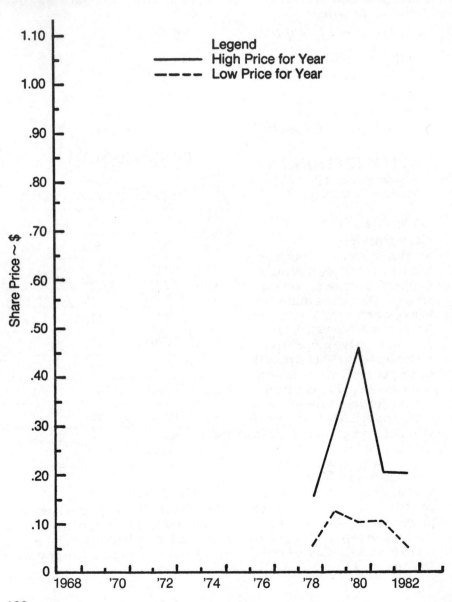

Spokane OTC
Inc. 1965
Washington

Silver King Mining & Milling Company

Route 2, Box 40
Usk, WA 99180
Pres. –Norman Junes
Sec. –Norman Haikkila

Transfer Agent:
Route 2, Box 40
Usk, WA 99180

CAPITALIZATION:
Capital stock authorized: 7,000,000 shares. Issued and outstanding: 5,229,439 shares.

DESCRIPTION OF COMPANY:
The company was organized to explore for silver and associated base metals in the Parker Lake Mining District of Pend Oreille County, Washington. In 1976, Silver King Mining Co. prospected and evaluated a uranium occurrence on a 72-claim (1320 acres) property in Mineral County, Nevada.

OPINION:
None.

PRICE HISTORY:

YEAR	HIGH	LOW
1978	.15	.05
1979	.30	.12
1980	.45	.10
1981	.20	.10
1982 to date	.20	.05

Silver Ledge Mining Company

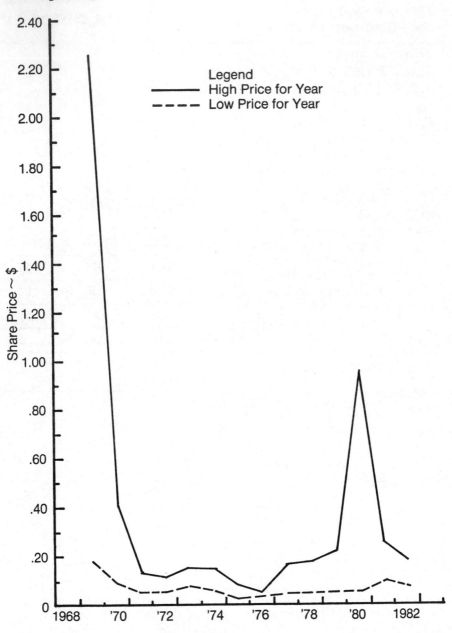

Share Price ~ $

Legend
—— High Price for Year
– – – Low Price for Year

Spokane Stock Exchange
Inc. 1966
Montana

Silver Ledge Mining Company

P.O. Box 488
111 N. 2nd St.
Coeur d'Alene, ID 83814
Pres. —Lee Revere
Sec. —Marvin W. Farmer

Transfer Agent:
P.O. Box 488
Coeur d'Alene, ID 83814

CAPITALIZATION:
Common stock, 10¢ par value; 8,000,000 authorized, 4,208,140 issued and outstanding.

DESCRIPTION OF COMPANY:
Has conducted mineral searches on properties in Montana and Oregon with negative results. Acquired 76 claims in Pend Oreille County, Washington, abandoned in 1979 after Denison Mines discontinued its exploration of the area for uranium. Now seeking properties of exploratory interest.

OPINION:
None.

PRICE HISTORY:

YEAR	HIGH	LOW
1969	2.25	.18
1970	.41	.09
1971	.13	.05
1972	.11	.05
1973	.15	.07
1974	.15	.05
1975	.08	.02
1976	.05	.03
1977	.16	.04
1978	.17	.04
1979	.22	.05
1980	.95	.05
1981	.25	.09
1982 to date	.18	.07

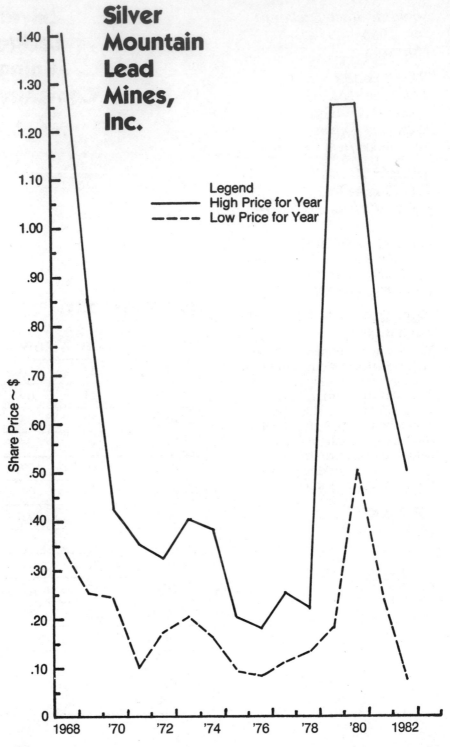

Silver Mountain Lead Mines, Inc.

Share Price ~ $

Legend
High Price for Year
Low Price for Year

1968 '70 '72 '74 '76 '78 '80 1982

Spokane Stock Exchange Inc. 1951 Idaho

834 McKinley Ave. Kellogg, ID 83837 Pres.–James Halley Sec.–Charles Hall

Transfer Agent: 834 McKinley Ave. Kellogg, ID 83837

Silver Mountain Lead Mines, Inc.

CAPITALIZATION:
Common, nonassessable capital stock, par value 10¢ per share; 3,066,000 shares issued and outstanding.

DESCRIPTION OF COMPANY:
Owns 160 acres of patented ground and 119 unpatented claims northeast of Mullan, Idaho. Neighbors include Lucky Friday, Vindicator, Princeton and Idaho-Montana Silver. Hecla and Bunker Hill spent more than $1.5 million on exploration in the 1950s. Only maintenance work since. Bunker Hill owns nearly 30% of outstanding shares.

OPINION:
One of the more attractive penny silver stocks because of its property holdings.

PRICE HISTORY:

YEAR	HIGH	LOW
1968	1.40	.33
1969	.85	.25
1970	.42	.24
1971	.35	.10
1972	.32	.17
1973	.40	.20
1974	.38	.16
1975	.20	.09
1976	.18	.08
1977	.25	.11
1978	.22	.13
1979	1.25	.18
1980	1.25	.50
1981	.75	.25
1982 to date	.50	.07

Silver Scott Mines, Inc.

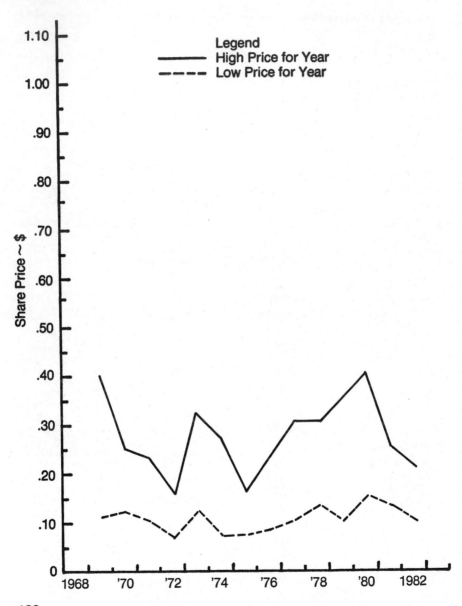

Spokane OTC
Inc. 1967
Idaho

P.O. Box 175
Leavenworth, WA 98826
Pres. – Earl A. Tenley
Sec./Treas. – Virginia
Tenley

Transfer Agent:
504 Bank St.
Box 1127
Wallace, ID 83873

Silver Scott Mines, Inc.

CAPITALIZATION:
Capital stock authorized: 4,990,000 shares, 20¢ par value, nonassessable. Issued and outstanding shares: 3,192,500.

DESCRIPTION OF COMPANY:
Organized to explore old Lost Cabin mine in old Murray gold camp, CDA District. Company expects Silver Scott's two main properties, the Moon Group in Moon Pass area south of Wallace at S.E. end of Silver Belt and the other Lost Cabin claims at Murray will eventually come under a major exploration and development program by a well financed major mining/oil company.

OPINION:
If a deal is made with a major company, Silver Scott's stock could work higher.

PRICE HISTORY:

YEAR	HIGH	LOW
1969	.40	.11
1970	.25	.12
1971	.23	.10
1972	.16	.07
1973	.32	.12
1974	.27	.07
1975	.16	.07
1976	.23	.08
1977	.30	.10
1978	.30	.13
1979	.35	.10
1980	.40	.15
1981	.25	.13
1982 to date	.21	.10

Silver Seal, Inc.

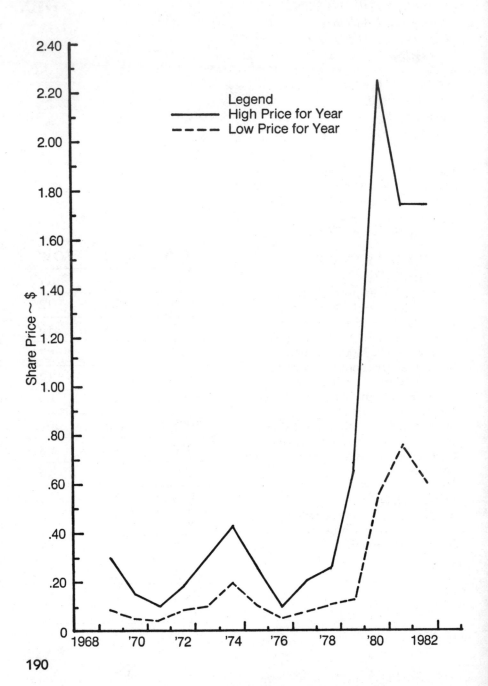

Spokane OTC
Inc. 1946
Idaho

2649 34th West
Seattle, WA 98199
Pres. – Vance D. McCarty
Sec. –Jeanne M. McCarty

Transfer Agent:
2649 34th West
Seattle, WA 98199

Silver Seal, Inc.

CAPITALIZATION:
5,000,000 shares of 10¢ par value stock capitalized; 3,269,088 shares issued and outstanding.

DESCRIPTION OF COMPANY:
Its original 27-claim property south of Sunshine mine, staked in the 1940s, has had limited exploration. In 1972, acquired Montana Gold Mountain Mining Co. whose property southwest of Butte yielded millions of dollars in gold in the 1870s. This property now undergoing test leaching by Montoro Gold, Inc., Vancouver, B.C. under 70/30 operating agreement signed in 1981. Old Spokane Molybdenum mine in Lincoln County, Washington, being test drilled by a U.S. Borax & Chemical subsidiary under a recently signed 70/30 operating agreement. Owns 100,000 shares of Silver Surprize and 60,000 shares of Gold Reserve Corporation.

OPINION:
Appears fully priced but could work higher on a substantial increase in silver.

PRICE HISTORY:

YEAR	HIGH	LOW
1969	.30	.08
1970	.15	.05
1971	.10	.04
1972	.18	.08
1973	.30	.10
1974	.42	.19
1975	.25	.10
1976	.10	.05
1977	.20	.07
1978	.25	.10
1979	.65	.12
1980	2.25	.55
1981	1.75	.75
1982 to date	1.75	.60

Silver Star Mines, Inc.

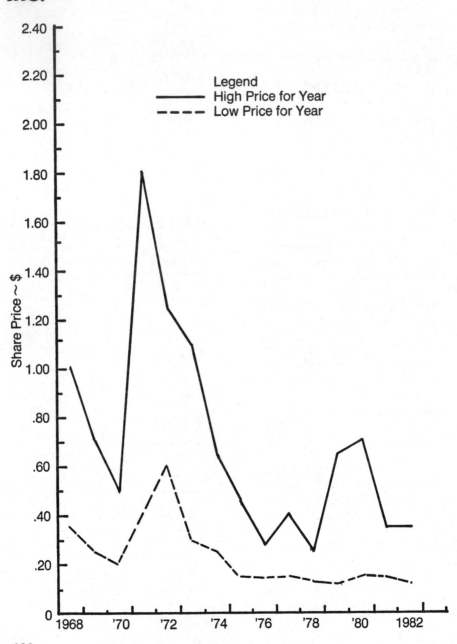

Spokane OTC
Inc. 1907
Idaho

P.O. Box 1025
Kellogg, ID 83837
Pres. –Philip G. Anderson
Sec. –Phyllis McKinnis

Transfer Agent:
Phyllis McKinnis
P.O. Box 1025
Kellogg, ID 83873

Silver Star Mines, Inc.

CAPITALIZATION:
Capital stock: authorized 3,000,000 shares of 10¢ par value nonassessable common stock, of which 2,094,503 shares are issued and outstanding.

DESCRIPTION OF COMPANY:
Owns 14 patented and 18 unpatented claims adjoining the closed Dayrock mine north of Wallace. Day Mines extended Dayrock workings into Silver Star ground in 1971 and mined silver-lead ore until 1974 when Dayrock ore reserves ran out and the mine shut down. Company negotiating to take over a Montana silver-lead mine.

OPINION:
Good properties; could do better with a major move in silver.

PRICE HISTORY:

YEAR	HIGH	LOW
1968	1.00	.35
1969	.70	.25
1970	.50	.20
1971	1.80	.40
1972	1.25	.60
1973	1.10	.30
1974	.65	.25
1975	.45	.15
1976	.28	.14
1977	.40	.15
1978	.25	.13
1979	.65	.12
1980	.70	.15
1981	.35	.15
1982 to date	.35	.12

Silver
Surprize,
Inc.

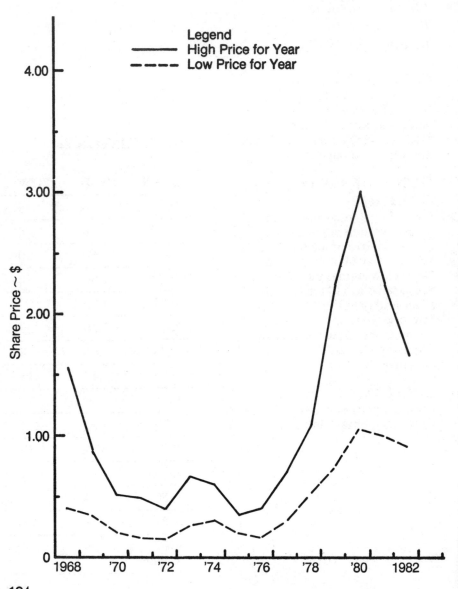

Spokane OTC
Inc. 1940
Idaho

2649 34th West
Seattle, WA 98199
Pres.—Vance D. McCarty
Sec.—Jeanne M. McCarty

Transfer Agent:
2649 34th West
Seattle, WA 98199

Silver Surprize, Inc.

CAPITALIZATION:
Common stock: authorized, 3,000,000 shares par value 5¢; issued and outstanding, 2,339,726 shares.

DESCRIPTION OF COMPANY:
Sandwiched between the Sunshine, Sunshine Consolidated and Metropolitan properties, its nine unpatented claims are subject to a 1946 50–50 profit-sharing operating agreement with Sunshine Mining Co. The latter followed a silver-bearing vein down into Silver Surprize ground claiming extralateral rights, but lost a lawsuit brought by Surprize for half of the ore and damages. Pending a judge's determination of damages, Sunshine offered to buy out Surprize shareholders for stock, but management awaits the court determination.

OPINION:
Underpriced at this writing. Shareholders will probably end up with cash or Sunshine stock.

PRICE HISTORY:

YEAR	HIGH	LOW
1968	1.55	.40
1969	.86	.35
1970	.52	.20
1971	.50	.15
1972	.40	.15
1973	.67	.25
1974	.61	.30
1975	.36	.20
1976	.41	.18
1977	.70	.30
1978	1.05	.52
1979	2.25	.75
1980	3.00	1.05
1981	2.25	1.00
1982 to date	1.65	.90

Silver Trend Mining Company

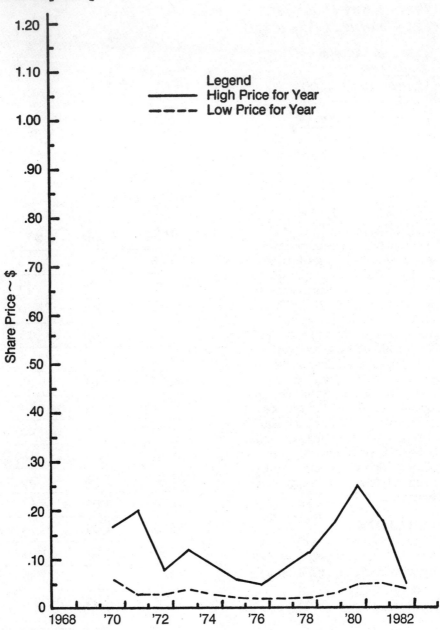

Spokane OTC
Inc. 1968
Idaho

P.O. Box 96
Kellogg, ID 83837
Pres.–Charles Asher
Sec./Treas.–Ronald E.
  Eggart

Transfer Agent:
P.O. Box 96
Kellogg, ID 83837

Silver Trend Mining Company

CAPITALIZATION:

Capital stock: authorized, 10,000,000 shares, par value 5¢ per share, of which 7,109,293 shares are issued and outstanding.

DESCRIPTION OF COMPANY:

In 1980 acquired Pyramid group of five unpatented claims in Churchill County, Nevada, from Nevada Rawhide Mining Co., and lessee has shipped some high-grade silver-gold development ore. Also acquired Nevada Rawhide's 11-claim Silver Bell property on Eddie Creek, Sanders County, Montana, and is doing limited exploration work. Has renewed lease on old Black Bear zinc-lead mine north of Wallace and plans further development when base metal prices improve.

OPINION:

Could be cheap if silver recovers substantially.

PRICE HISTORY:

YEAR	HIGH	LOW
1970	.17	.06
1971	.20	.03
1972	.08	.03
1973	.12	.04
1974	.09	.03
1975	.06	.02
1976	.05	.02
1977	.06	.02
1978	.12	.02
1979	.17	.03
1980	.25	.05
1981	.18	.05
1982 to date	.05	.04

Silver Verde May Mining Company

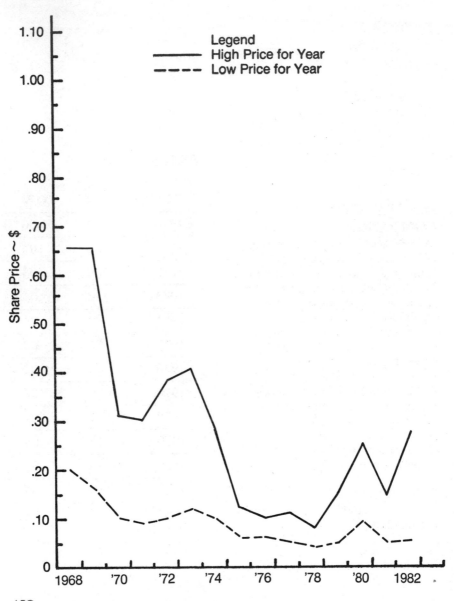

Spokane OTC
Inc. 1906
Idaho

413 Cedar St.
Wallace, ID 83873
Pres. – William Zanetti
Sec. – R.M. MacPhee

Transfer Agent:
H.F. Magnuson & Co.
P.O. Box 469
Wallace, ID 83873

Silver Verde May Mining Company

CAPITALIZATION:
Capital stock, par value 5¢ per share, authorized 2,000,000 shares, of which 1,991,905 shares are issued and outstanding.

DESCRIPTION OF COMPANY:
Six unpatented claims in Burke Canyon, 2 miles north of Wallace, adjoining the Canyon Silver. A joint exploration was in progress until the Seattle operators encountered difficulties. In 1972 signed agreement with Canyon Silver Mines for exploration of Verde ground. Also has large cash position.

OPINION:
Appears to be one of the cheaper penny stocks with good potential. Because of its small capitalization Verde May could move faster than some of the others.

PRICE HISTORY:

YEAR	HIGH	LOW
1968	.65	.20
1969	.65	.16
1970	.31	.10
1971	.30	.09
1972	.38	.10
1973	.40	.12
1974	.28	.10
1975	.12	.06
1976	.10	.06
1977	.11	.05
1978	.08	.04
1979	.15	.05
1980	.25	.09
1981	.15	.05
1982 to date	.27	.05

Silverore Mines, Inc.

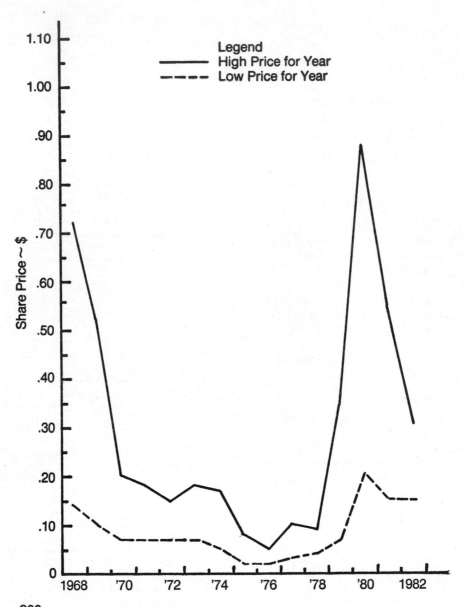

Spokane OTC
Inc. 1946
Idaho

P.O. Box 487
Portland, OR 97207
(503) 227-3277
Pres. – W.T. Anderson
Sec. – Burton W. Onstine

Transfer Agent:
Burton W. Onstine
P.O. Box 487
Portland, OR 97207

Silverore Mines, Inc.

CAPITALIZATION:
5,000,000 common shares authorized; 3,683,426 shares issued and outstanding.

DESCRIPTION OF COMPANY:
Silverore Mines, Inc. owns 10 patented and 10 unpatented mining claims in the Evolution and Beaver Mining Districts in Shoshone County, Idaho. Inspiration Lead Company, Inc. owns one patented and 35 unpatented mining claims in the same mining district. Silverore and Inspiration entered into an agreement to divide 50–50 all ore discovered on these 56 claims. Sunshine Mining Company, in 1979, entered into a revised exploration agreement covering the company's 20 claims and Inspiration Lead Company's 36 claims. Sunshine Mining Co. after completion of the diamond drill hole on February 27, 1981, has not performed any further exploration or development work on the company properties. Other companies in the area have

PRICE HISTORY:

YEAR	HIGH	LOW
1968	.72	.14
1969	.52	.10
1970	.20	.07
1971	.18	.07
1972	.15	.07
1973	.18	.07
1974	.17	.05
1975	.08	.02
1976	.05	.02
1977	.10	.03
1978	.09	.04
1979	.35	.07
1980	.88	.20
1981	.55	.15
1982 to date	.30	.15

indicated an interest in further exploration of the companies' property in a joint venture type operation with Sunshine, but no formal agreements have been formulated.

OPINION:
Certainly one of the more attractive penny stocks because of Sunshine's association.

201

Square Deal Mining & Milling Company

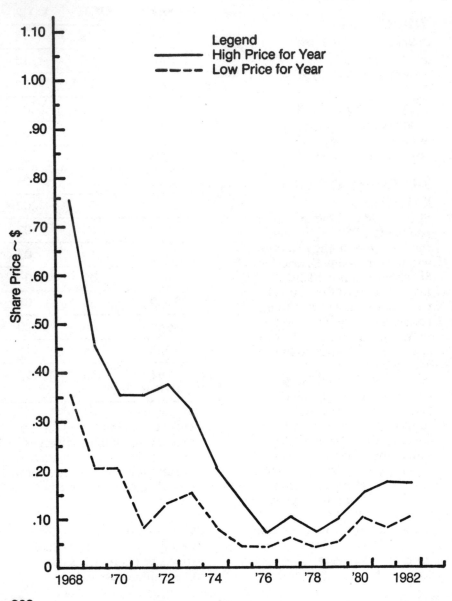

Spokane OTC
Inc. 1906
Idaho

P.O. Box 469
Wallace, ID 83873
Pres. – Wray Featherstone
Sec. – D.L. Hess

Transfer Agent:
H.F. Magnuson & Co.
P.O. Box 469
Wallace, ID 83873

Square Deal Mining & Milling Company

CAPITALIZATION:
2,000,000 shares of authorized nonassessable, capital stock with a par value of 10¢ per share. As of December 31, 1981, there were 1,835,989 shares of stock issued and outstanding.

DESCRIPTION OF COMPANY:
Owns 16 claims northeast of Wallace surrounded by the Golconda and Alice Consolidated groups of claims. Exploration from Golconda mine's 1,800-foot level in the 1950s opened several small shoots of zinc ore, but they were not mined. Annual assessment work only at present. Owns 349,600 shares Alice Consolidated Mines, Inc.

OPINION:
One of many penny silver stocks that would automatically move up in price with a big increase in the price of silver.

PRICE HISTORY:

YEAR	HIGH	LOW
1968	.75	.35
1969	.45	.20
1970	.35	.20
1971	.35	.08
1972	.37	.13
1973	.32	.15
1974	.20	.08
1975	.13	.04
1976	.07	.04
1977	.10	.06
1978	.07	.04
1979	.10	.05
1980	.15	.10
1981	.17	.08
1982 to date	.17	.10

Sterling Mining Company

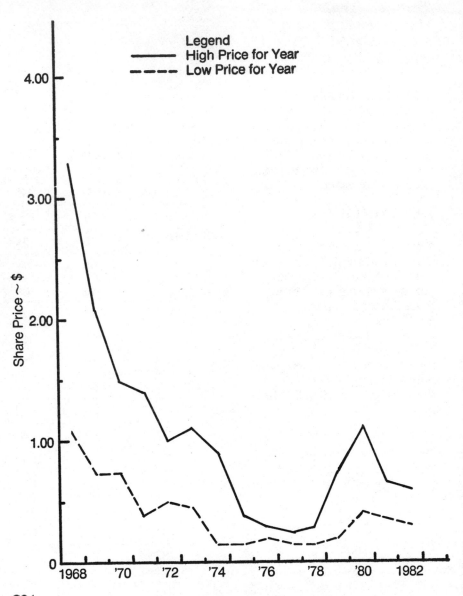

Sterling Mining Company

414 River St.
Wallace, ID 83873
Pres. – Frank McKinley

Transfer Agent:
P.O. Box 889
Wallace, ID 83873

CAPITALIZATION:
5,000,000 shares of nonassessable common stock with a par value of 5¢ per share. 3,083,894 shares issued and outstanding.

DESCRIPTION OF COMPANY:
Holds a long east-west strip of 15 claims bordering on the south Callahan Mining's Galena mine property and the ASARCO-Hecla-owned Triangle group. Western portion leased years ago by owners of Triangle but no development being done. Lease on eastern portion terminated by ASARCO in 1977.

OPINION:
One of the more attractive smaller silver stocks in a rising silver market.

PRICE HISTORY:

YEAR	HIGH	LOW
1968	3.25	1.10
1969	2.10	.75
1970	1.50	.75
1971	1.40	.40
1972	1.00	.50
1973	1.10	.45
1974	.90	.15
1975	.40	.15
1976	.30	.20
1977	.25	.15
1978	.30	.15
1979	.75	.20
1980	1.10	.40
1981	.65	.35
1982 to date	.60	.30

Summit
Silver
Inc.

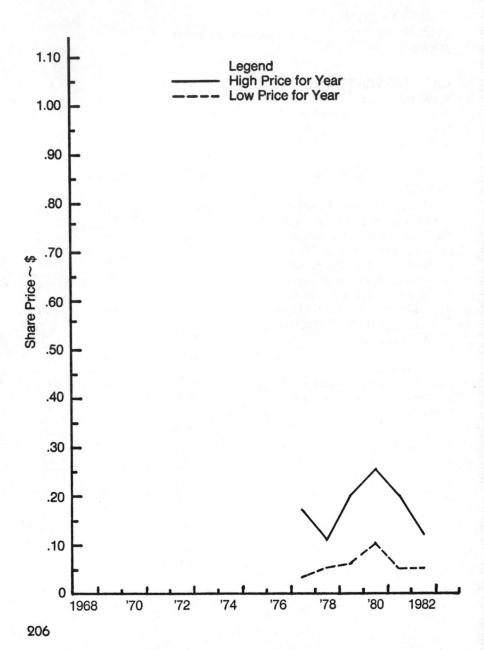

Spokane OTC
Inc. 1968
Idaho

Suite 202
111 North 2nd St.
Coeur d'Alene, ID 83814
Pres. –Peter Laczay

Transfer Agent:
P.O. Box 488
Coeur d'Alene, ID 83814

Summit Silver Inc.

CAPITALIZATION:
5,000,000 shares of 10¢ par value stock; 4,217,793 shares were issued and 781,350 shares reserved for conversion by the former Kimberly Gold Mines, Inc. shareholders.

DESCRIPTION OF COMPANY:
Owns former Kimberly Gold Mines, Inc., property east of Riggins, Idaho, being developed by Gold Resources, Inc., under 1979 operating agreement entitling Summit to 40% of net operating profits and $3 per ton rental on use of Kimberly flotation mill. Also owns Baltimore mine, former silver-copper producer, near Boulder, Montana, and a 60-claim copper-silver prospect just across the Montana border east of Mullan, IDaho. Owns 93,000 shares of Idora Silver Mines, Inc. and 186,000 shares of Champion Gold and Silver.

OPINION:
None.

PRICE HISTORY:

YEAR	HIGH	LOW
1977	.17	.03
1978	.11	.05
1979	.20	.06
1980	.25	.10
1981	.20	.05
1982 to date	.12	.05

Sunshine Mining Company

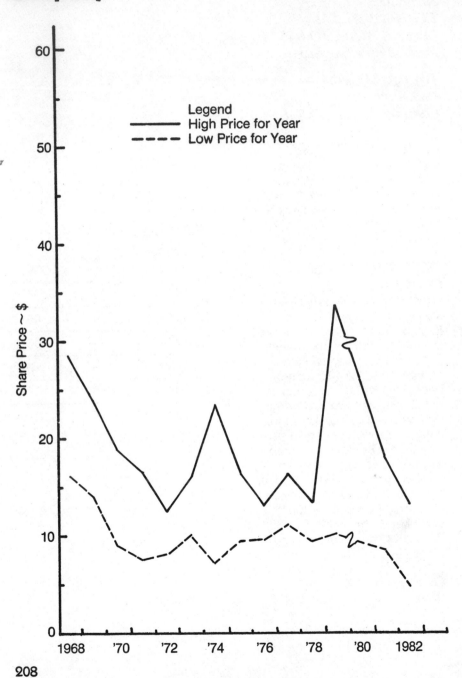

Legend
——— High Price for Year
- - - - Low Price for Year

Share Price ~ $

60

50

40

30

20

10

0

1968 '70 '72 '74 '76 '78 '80 1982

New York Stock Exchange
Spokane Stock Exchange
Inc. 1921
Idaho

Sunshine Mining Company

500 Plaza of the
*   Americas-South*
Dallas, TX 75201
Pres. –G. Michael Boswell
Sec. –Harry B. Ireland, Jr.

Transfer Agent:
National Bank of
*   Commerce (common*
*   stock)*
P.O. Box 568
Dallas, TX 75221
Continental Illinois
*   National Bank and*
*   Trust Co. (Silver Indexed*
*   Bonds)*
30 North La Salle St.
Chicago, IL 60693

CAPITALIZATION:
Comon stock par value 50¢ per share, authorized 50,000,000 shares; 22,925,484 issued and outstanding.

SPECIAL NOTE:
The remainder of long term debt outstanding on December 31, 1981 and 1980, consists of 8½% silver-indexed bonds, $30,000,000 (less current portion of $2,100,000) due April 15, 1995, and $27,500,000 (less current portion of $1,925,000) due December 15, 1995. Capitalized bond issue costs of $3,667,000 are being amortized over the life of the bonds. Each $1,000 face bond is payable at maturity or redemption at the greater of

PRICE HISTORY:

YEAR	HIGH	LOW
1968	28.50	16.00
1969	24.00	14.00
1970	18.75	9.00
1971	16.50	7.50
1972	12.50	8.00
1973	16.00	10.00
1974	23.25	7.25
1975	16.25	9.25
1976	13.00	9.50
1977	16.00	11.00
1978	13.25	9.25
1979	33.55	10.00
1980	*26.00	9.00
1981	18.00	8.00
1982 to date	13.00	4.65

*Adjusted for 50% stock split

209

$1,000 or a specified market price of 50 ounces of silver (the "Indexed Principal Amount").

DESCRIPTION OF COMPANY:

The Sunshine mine in the Coeur d'Alene Mining District's Silver Belt contains the largest known silver ore body in the U.S. and possibly the world. Ore reserves are estimated at more than 100 million ounces. Production in 1981 was 1,144,732 ounces, and Sunshine's silver refinery became operational. The neighboring Silver Dollar, Silver Syndicate, Sunshine Consolidated and Big Creek Apex properties were acquired in a $50 million transaction. A Nevada silver mine was placed on stream and a Utah silver-lead-zinc mine readied for production. Sunshine increased its interest in the Consolidated Silver property south of Osburn, Idaho, to 29%.

OPINION:

Belongs in every large silver stock portfolio at this time.

BIG CREEK APEX MINING COMPANY

Effective December 30, 1981 Big Creek Apex Mining Company was acquired by Sunshine Mining Company on the basis of 71½ shares of Sunshine for 100 shares of Big Creek Apex.

SILVER DOLLAR MINING COMPANY

Effective December 30, 1981 Silver Dollar Mining Company was acquired by Sunshine Mining Company on the basis of 115 shares of Sunshine for 100 shares of Silver Dollar.

SILVER SYNDICATE INC.

Effective December 30, 1981 Silver Syndicate Inc. was acquired by Sunshine Mining Company on the basis of 75 shares of Sunshine for 100 shares of Silver Syndicate.

SUNSHINE CONSOLIDATED, INC.

Effective December 30, 1981 Sunshine Consolidated, Inc. was acquired by Sunshine Mining Company on the basis of 55 shares of Sunshine for 100 shares of Sunshine Consolidated.

Sunshine silver "Round" minted by Sunshine Mining Company is the equivalent in silver to the Krugerrand in gold. More than 500,000 have been produced and sold. "Rounds" are sold through major coin dealers.

Superior
Silver
Mines
Inc.

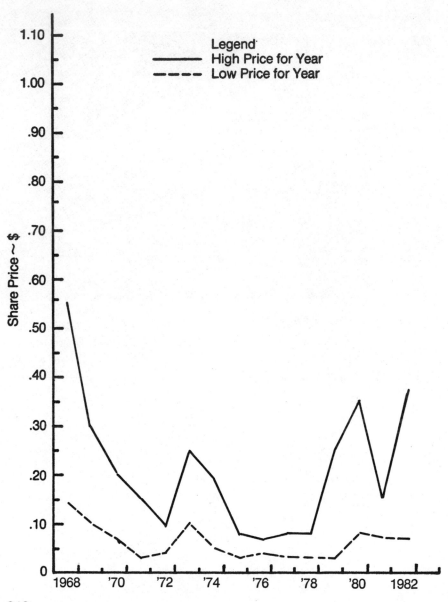

Spokane OTC
Inc. 1962

12019 East Sprague Ave.
Spokane, WA 99206
Pres. – T.S. Smith

Transfer Agent:
12019 East Sprague Ave.
Spokane, WA 99206

Superior Silver Mines Inc.

CAPITALIZATION:
Capital stock, par value 10¢ per share, authorized 10,000,000 shares, issued and outstanding 5,678,934 shares.

DESCRIPTION OF COMPANY:
Owns 55 claims in the Superior, Montana, area, leased to Nancy Lee Mines in 1967 and currently subleased to Western Silver Development Co.; 12 claims south of Mullan adjoining Atlas group on south. Announced agreement between Bear Creek Mining Company and Anaconda Minerals Company providing for the exploration of nine mining claims located in east Shoshone County, Idaho, south of the Lucky Friday Mine. By this agreement, Bear Creek Mining Co., a division of the Kennecott Corp., has assigned its lessee's interest in the mining claims to Anaconda Minerals. Anaconda is a division of Atlantic Richfield.

OPINION:
Interest has come into Superior because of ARCO (Anaconda) Exploration agreement. Could work higher on a better silver market also.

PRICE HISTORY:

YEAR	HIGH	LOW
1968	.55	.14
1969	.30	.10
1970	.20	.07
1971	.15	.03
1972	.10	.04
1973	.25	.10
1974	.19	.05
1975	.08	.03
1976	.07	.04
1977	.08	.03
1978	.08	.03
1979	.25	.03
1980	.35	.08
1981	.15	.07
1982 to date	.37	.07

United Mines, Inc.

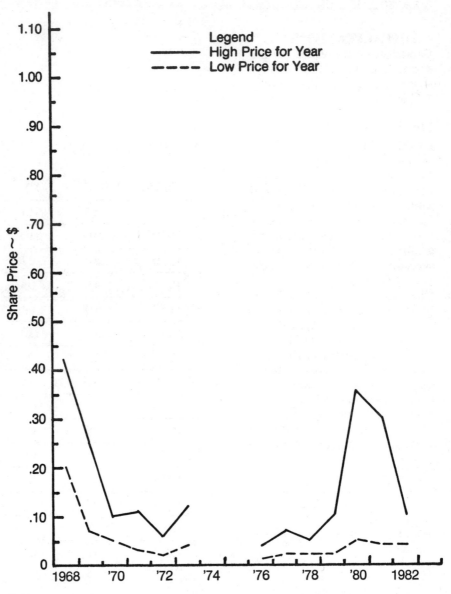

Spokane OTC
Inc. 1947
Idaho

P.O. Box 668
Coeur d'Alene, ID 83814
Pres. – Stanley Harrison

Transfer Agent:
P.O. Box 668
Coeur d'Alene, ID 83814

United Mines, Inc.

CAPITALIZATION:
Capital stock 1,000,000
common stock class "A,"
5,000,000 common stock class
"B." All have been issued.

DESCRIPTION OF COMPANY:
Three-claim property just north
of Silver Syndicate group now
owned by Sunshine Mining was
leased to Sunshine in 1980 for
35% of profits if commercial ore
found and advance royalties of
$3,500 yearly, increasing to
$5,000 in 1985. In 1968
acquired 15 claims near head of
Big Creek south of Wallace.

OPINION:
Although their property is small,
it is well located near Sunshine
and in up markets the stock is
attractive.

PRICE HISTORY:

YEAR	HIGH	LOW
1968	.41	.20
1969	.25	.07
1970	.10	.05
1971	.11	.03
1972	.06	.02
1973	.12	.04
1974		
1975		
1976	.04	.01
1977	.07	.02
1978	.05	.02
1979	.10	.02
1980	.35	.05
1981	.30	.04
1982 to date	.10	.04

Utah-Idaho
Consolidated,
Inc.

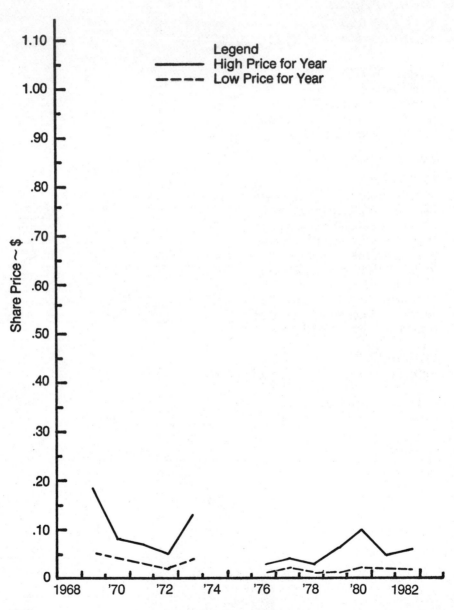

Spokane OTC
Inc. 1954
Idaho

Utah-Idaho Consolidated, Inc.

P.O. Box 668
Coeur d'Alene, ID 83814
Pres. – Stanley Harrison

Transfer Agent:
P.O. Box 668
Coeur d'Alene, ID 83814

CAPITALIZATION:
Capital stock, authorized
10,000,000 shares of common
stock with a par value of 10¢ per
share, all of which have been
issued.

DESCRIPTION OF COMPANY:
Ten claims south of the Silver
Bowl property on Big Creek and
14 claims, 4 miles south of
Wallace, Idaho.

OPINION:
None.

PRICE HISTORY:

YEAR	HIGH	LOW
1969	.18	.05
1970	.08	.04
1971	.07	.03
1972	.05	.02
1973	.13	.04
1974		
1975		
1976	.03	.01
1977	.04	.02
1978	.03	.01
1979	.06	.01
1980	.10	.02
1981	.05	.02
1982 to date	.06	.02

Vindicator
Silver
Lead
Mining
Company

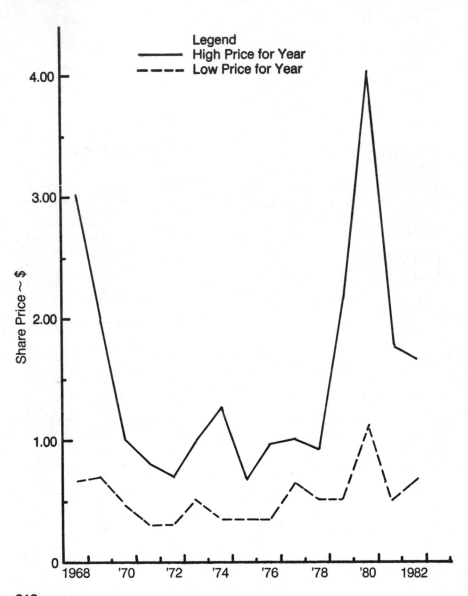

Spokane OTC
Inc. 1902
Idaho

P.O. Box 469
Wallace, ID 83873
Pres.–H.F. Magnuson
Sec.–D.L. Hess

Transfer Agent:
H.F. Magnuson & Co.
P.O. Box 469
Wallace, ID 83873

Vindicator Silver Lead Mining Company

CAPITALIZATION:

4,000,000 shares of authorized nonassessable, capital stock with a par value of 10¢ per share; 3,812,820 shares of stock issued and outstanding.

DESCRIPTION OF COMPANY:

Owns one patented and five un-patented claims bordering Hecla's Lucky Friday mine property on the north. Developed by 800-foot shaft put down in 1950s by Silver Buckle Mining Co., which owns about 900,000 Vindicator shares.

OPINION:

It is anticipated that Hecla may possibly wish to explore Vindicator, and the prospect of deep exploration of the area surrounding the Lucky Friday Mine has brought renewed interest in the shares of Vindicator.

PRICE HISTORY:

YEAR	HIGH	LOW
1968	3.00	.67
1969	2.00	.70
1970	1.00	.46
1971	.80	.30
1972	.70	.30
1973	1.00	.50
1974	1.25	.35
1975	.65	.35
1976	.95	.35
1977	1.00	.65
1978	.90	.50
1979	2.15	.50
1980	4.00	1.10
1981	1.75	.50
1982 to date	1.65	.65

Western Silver Lead

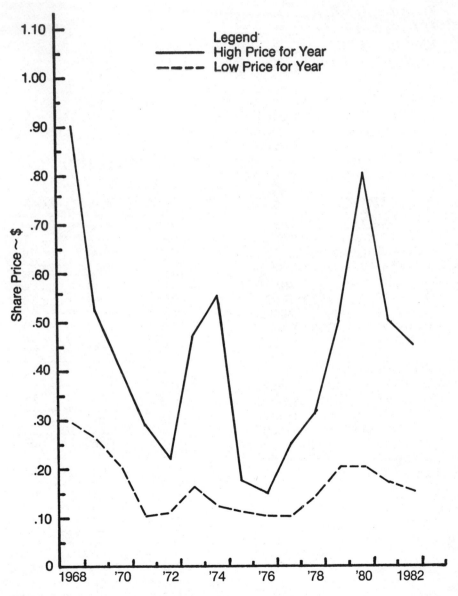

Spokane Stock Exchange Inc. 1947
Idaho

413 Cedar St.
Wallace, ID 83873
Pres. – George Grismer
Sec. – D.L. Hess

Transfer Agent:
P.O. Box 469
Wallace, ID 83873

Western Silver Lead

CAPITALIZATION:

Class A common capital stock: nonassessable, par value 5¢ per share, authorized 1,200,000 shares, of which 946,529 shares are issued and outstanding. Class B common capital stock: assessable, par value 5¢ per share, authorized 2,400,000 shares, of which 1,816,384 shares are issued.

DESCRIPTION OF COMPANY:

Organized to explore 12 unpatented claims and 14 acres of patented ground less than 2 miles east of Wallace. Drove 1,050-foot adit and found lead-silver mineralization. On standby basis in recent years. Also owns 25% interest in nine-claim Phoenix uranium prospect in San Juan County, Utah, and 45,000 shares of Sunshine Mining.

OPINION:

Both A and B stocks have been attractive in this current market and interest could continue with higher silver prices.

PRICE HISTORY:

Class A Stock

YEAR	HIGH	LOW
1968	.90	.29
1969	.52	.26
1970	.41	.20
1971	.29	.10
1972	.22	.11
1973	.47	.16
1974	.55	.12
1975	.17	.11
1976	.15	.10
1977	.25	.10
1978	.31	.14
1979	.50	.20
1980	.80	.20
1981	.50	.17
1982 to date	.45	.15

221

Western
Silver
Lead

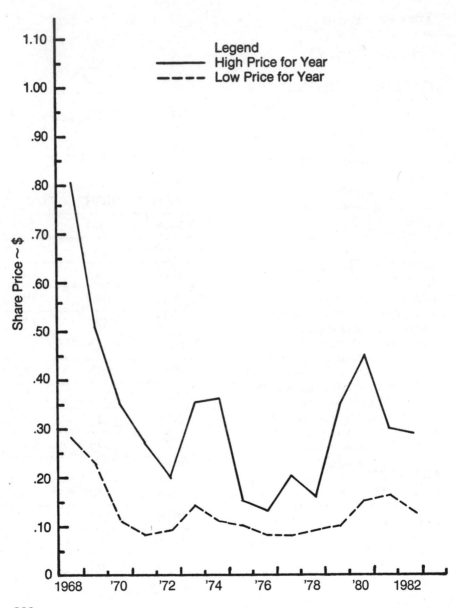

Western
Silver
Lead

PRICE HISTORY:

Class B Stock

YEAR	HIGH	LOW
1968	.80	.28
1969	.51	.23
1970	.35	.11
1971	.27	.08
1972	.20	.09
1973	.35	.14
1974	.36	.11
1975	.15	.10
1976	.13	.08
1977	.20	.08
1978	.16	.09
1979	.35	.10
1980	.45	.15
1981	.30	.16
1982 to date	.29	.13

Yreka
United
Inc.

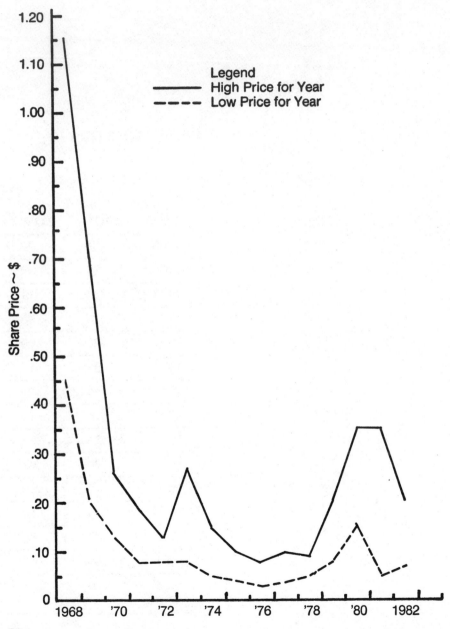

Spokane OTC
Inc. 1898
Idaho

P.O. Box 147
Kellogg, ID 83837
Pres. –Earl T. Siler

Transfer Agent:
P.O. Box 147
Kellogg, ID 83837

Yreka United Inc.

CAPITALIZATION:
Capital stock, authorized
7,500,000 shares with a par
value of 10¢ per share, of which
6,538,021 are issued and outstanding.

DESCRIPTION OF COMPANY:
Owns 26 patented and 49
unpatented claims adjacent to
Bunker Hill claims south of
Kellogg. Under Bunker Hill
working agreement, Yreka
would receive 50% of ores produced in one area and 25% in
another. Four unpatented claims
in nearby Pine Creek sector
under 50–50 agreement with
Signal Silver-Gold which recently leased its Pine Creek holdings
to Cominco American.

OPINION:
At this writing definitely one of
the attractive penny silver stocks
in the CDA Mining Region.

PRICE HISTORY:

YEAR	HIGH	LOW
1968	1.15	.45
1969	.70	.20
1970	.26	.13
1971	.19	.08
1972	.13	.08
1973	.27	.08
1974	.15	.05
1975	.10	.04
1976	.08	.03
1977	.10	.04
1978	.09	.05
1979	.20	.08
1980	.35	.15
1981	.35	.05
1982 to date	.20	.07

APPENDIX

The following publications are invaluable for those wishing to gain additional understanding and background and to keep current on the silver situation.

Books

Silver Profits in the 80's
 Jerome F. Smith
 Copyright 1982, Books in Focus, Inc.,
 P.O. Box 3481, Grand Central Station,
 New York, NY 10163

The Silver Bulls
 Paul Sarnoff
 Copyright 1980, Paul Sarnoff,
 120 Broadway - 7th Floor, Commodities -
 Metals Dept., New York, NY 10271

Market & Investment Letters

International Moneyline
 Julian M. Snyder
 25 Broad St., New York, NY 10004

Green's Commodity Letter
 Charles Stahl
 Economic News Agency, Inc., P.O. Box 174,
 Princeton, NJ 08540

The Silver & Gold Report
 David Rosenthal
 Precious Metals Report, Inc., P.O. Box 325,
 Newtown, CT 06470

Let's Talk Silver & Gold
 James Sibbet
 Sibbet Publications, 61 South Lake Ave.,
 Pasadena, CA 91101

INDEX

Index